Everybody Knows:

The Power of Being in Position

Praise for *Everybody Knows: The Power of Being in Position*

"*Everybody Knows* is a raw account of the revelation process of one of God's great gifts, purpose. Georgia is authentic, honest, and pointed in sharing the truth that is needed to spark a movement of purpose in herself and others. *Everybody Knows* is an invitation that if you don't think you're invited, it's because you aren't listening."

— Jazmin M. Caton, EdD
Independent Researcher & Educational Services Consultant

"I highly recommend this book not just for my patients but for anyone struggling with past, traumatic events. This book illustrates how one can overcome tragedy and use it to recover, not just for self-help but also to help others going through similar challenges. Ms. Georgia is a solid example of how not to allow your past to dictate your future."

— Dr. Ganielle Hooper
Certified Pediatric Mental Health Specialist

"In this book, Ms. Dawkins encourages each of us to find our paths and get into position not only for ourselves, but so we may also help propel our fellow neighbor forward on their simultaneous journey to inner peace and fulfillment. If you find that you are living in fear, or not quite walking in your purpose, this book is highly recommended as it may provide the assistance you need to make the next major decision in your life.?

— Dr. Tressa D. Stiles
Licensed Psychologist

"Everybody Knows isn't just a book; it's a journey."

— Brandy Stinson
Clinical Social Work/Therapist, MSW, LCSW, MAC

Copyright © 2018, 2019 Georgia Dawkins

Cover Design by Modern Mission
Author Photograph by Tyrone Myrick
Creative Direction by Sheldon G. Horton
Published by Georgia Dawkins Media, LLC
Editing by Marti Covington

Scripture taken from Holy Bible, New International Version
Printed in the United States of America

Second Edition
ISBN-13: 978-0-692-17112-7

First Edition
ISBN: 0578204223

Printed in the United States of America

www.GeorgiaDawkins.com

Contents

For Georgia Mae, Lizzie, Track, Dolly and Leotis

Everybody Knows:

The Power of Being in Position

Georgia Dawkins

Forward

I first met Georgia Dawkins as a high school student with a passion to write. She walked in my office with a contagious smile spread across her face and the kind of enthusiasm that an editor looks for in any potential writer.

I have watched her grow, first as her editor at the local newspaper, and now from afar as she continues to spread her wings and fly to new horizons, never skipping a beat. This book, "Everybody Knows: The Power of Being in Position," tells her story.

From a small coffee shop in Tampa to Tybee Island near Savannah, Georgia spent a short nine days in solitude to write her story. What started as words being put to paper during one of the darkest chapters of her life has turned into a book that Georgia said has not only healed her, but has healed others who have read it.

Everybody Knows is about Georgia's life. A life that has had a lot of tragedy and trauma, some of it during her early childhood. It is a book about "learning to see signs that are specifically designed for those of us who are 'in the world and not of the world.' "

In these pages, Georgia shares her innermost secrets and her victories, her fears and her joy. All things made possible and celebrated because of her love from God and of herself.

She proudly points to the book cover, a picture of her smaller self, and says "This girl is still ministering to this girl (pointing to herself)." And through that ministering, Georgia turns it around to help others learn to trust in their Father.

From a high school student looking to write about the community she grew up in to a broadcast producer, she has been honored as one of the most promising young journalist students in the country.

In 2014, Georgia was named one of six Diversity Leadership Fellows by the Society of Professional Journalists, and the Journalism and Women Symposium (JAWS) selected her as one of 10 "Emerging Journalists." She has also been honored by the National Association of Black Journalists for Outstanding Literary Work.

Before every new chapter of her life she has written, she says she always comes back home. She calls our small community her spiritual foundation, a reflection of who she is.

Take some time for yourself and read Georgia's book. You won't be disappointed and you'll quickly learn why her community stands proudly behind her.

Romona D. Washington
Executive Editor, Highlands News-Sun

PREFACE

This book is about purpose.

I am on the road to finding mine. I wrote this book so anyone who reads it can see the vulnerability of my walk. I also want them to see that God can use anyone. It doesn't matter if you're gay, drunk, high or just distracted right now. When God says move, you get into position.

I'm moving into position now. It is coming about as a series of decisions. Some were divine, others were choices. My move started when I sat down to write this book. I did it when I left what I thought was my dream job. Neither move was easy. Getting into position means that someone — probably you — might be uncomfortable for a period of time. But situating yourself where God wants you to be is a liberating experience.

Getting into position gave me a truth about myself I had trouble accepting.

I am a light, and no matter what I do or where I go, my purpose finds me. The book you are about to read explains how I tried to ignore my purpose in a variety of ways.

If I can do nothing else well, I can find a distraction. Sometimes the distraction is a toxic job. Sometimes the distraction is ordering delivery just so I can waste time eating a meal that I will carry around on my body for years. Then there are times when the distraction is downloading a dating app just to waste time that I know I will never get back. Anything that robs you of your creativity or your energy is a distraction.

I've learned that your distractions affect more than just you.

What's alarming is someone somewhere else is waiting on you to make a decision that could change their life. I am not here to judge you. In order to do that, I'd have to first judge myself and my God tells me that's not my job. Just let my story be a reminder that people are waiting on your gifts. They are depending on you to get into position so that they can make their next best move.

This book is not about putting my business in the streets. This book is like my life. It's about what God did and is doing – all while putting me in a position to be properly prepared for what comes next.

When my mother tells the suspense thriller about the night I was born, she tells me how she couldn't move until I got into position.

I believe that's what God is saying to us. *I cannot move until you get in position.*

This book is about what happens afterward. I know from experience that the events birthed after painful transitions are more wonderful than any of us can imagine.

– 1 –
MOTHER'S DAY

Getting into position requires a lot of mental preparation. Ask Usain Bolt. Yeah, he only runs for 11 seconds, but how much time did he spend in his head prepping for those 50-yard, record-setting dashes? This book is about me getting in position to fulfill divine assignments. I know that sounds arrogant.

Just read. It isn't.

> "Before I formed you in the womb I knew you. Before you were born I set you apart; I appointed you as a prophet to the nations."
> — Jeremiah 1:5 NIV

The position I am moving toward started with my name. I was named after two women in my family who lived and died before I was born. My name is also the title of one of America's favorite songs made popular by a blind singer from the South. Most people know the song and sing it to me when they hear my name. As you can probably imagine, "Georgia on my mind" is a song that I don't go a day without hearing. The song is one reason I grew up despising my government name. But the more I learn about the women in my family who wore it before me, the more I realize it is an honor to continue the legacy.

I am Georgia from Florida. That's the headline I use when introducing myself to a crowd for the first time. It's catchy! I like it. I am a leader in development and it seems I always have been. Though she didn't realize it at the time, even my mother knew while she carried me that I innately knew the value of getting in position. It started before my birth. It's a story that involves my whole family.

The way my mama explains it is so special that I only ask her to tell it once a year. It's like "The Night Before Christmas" without the sugar plums or the fat white man breaking into your home. This story features a bloodied 8-year-old boy, a payphone, a neighbor, my dad, foot stitches and a bicycle.

Every time I hear this story, it reminds me of my destiny. As I write this book I know I am full-term and ready to give birth to my dreams.

In October, toward the end of the 80s, my older brother ran to my mom's apartment door with blood-soaked pants. My mom is beyond dramatic, so she immediately thought somebody raped him.

"Who did it? Who did it?" She asked him.

Through his tears, he explained that he'd cut his foot climbing a tree. But it was more than just a cut; it was a two-inch wide gash in his foot. My dad was on "The Corner" a half mile away from the Martin Luther King Terrace where we lived. The Corner was never empty. It was the only place in our community to shoot dice, catch up with classmates, score dope or grab a pickled pig's foot. Mom first called the payphone closest to his hangout, but there was no answer.

So, being the amazingly dramatic mother that she is, she borrowed a bicycle and rode down a hill to find him. Remember, I'm inside her belly and have been there for nine months. Once she laid eyes on him, she threw the bicycle in the car and raced back to the apartment.

Great, mom! Just forget the fact you could drop a baby at any moment.

My older brother has always been her favorite.

"That's my tiny, tiny baby," she once tried to convince me. "He will always be my tiny, tiny baby. I don't know what y'all gon' do when I leave here, but y'all hold him up."

I will never stop telling people that I hold the title of favorite, though. I mean, hey, I am the only girl of four children. I win by default.

Back to my birth.

My mother then rushed to the emergency room where she nearly passed out while they stitched up my brother's foot. She spent the whole day at the hospital just to come back home and go into labor.

"When I came back home, I went for a walk," she says.

Nine months pregnant and walking? I know, right?

She decided to stroll over to Cottie Mae's house. She's a family friend who lived in a house adjacent to "The Terrace," as it was called.

"When I got up there, that's when you decided to get into position," she reflected.

This is the part where she explains how I rolled around inside of her, pushing on her ribs and disrupting her peace.

"I didn't even realize you were in position to come out."

This revelation always puzzled me because it's not like I was her first child. I am still a little confused about how she didn't recognize the signs.

"I thought I had peed on myself, so I changed my underwear, went back inside and I said, 'Dog, I peed in my clothes again.'"

She said she changed her underwear three times before calling the doctors. I guess it's like she's always told me, "If you weren't Black, you'd be blonde."

I'm not sure how to take that coming from my mom, but I'm sure it sounds just as insulting coming from a stranger.

She and I are more alike than she thinks.

" "

YOU DIDN'T MISS OUT ON THE
OPPORTUNITY BECAUSE YOU
WEREN'T GOOD ENOUGH.
YOU WERE BEING PROTECTED
BECAUSE GOD KNEW YOU
WERE TOO GOOD FOR THE THING
YOU TRIED TO SETTLE FOR.

– GEORGIA DAWKINS –

EVERYBODY
KNOWS:
THE POWER OF BEING IN POSITION

After she spoke to the doctor, she decided to wait awhile before going in. Then, a thunderstorm came, and I wasn't too far behind.

I don't know how, but each time she tells this story, I learn a little more about mama and a lot more about God. He can't move until we're in position, and every labor pain brings us one step closer to giving birth.

After I was born, family lore turned into regular family life – starting with how I was named.

Once upon a time, we had a tradition in our family where the men would name the children. Most of my cousins have Middle Eastern names. Everyone's name has a meaning. So, when it came down to naming me, the source was the same but the result was not. Mom picked up the phone and called her big sister.

"I had the baby," she announced. "It's a girl. What should I name her?"

Auntie Teedy turned to Uncle Leotis and said, "Jerm had the baby. It's a girl. She needs a name."

It always baffles me that after 30 years of listening to this story, there was never a "congratulations!" My family is weird.

He rolled over and responded, "Georgia Elizabeth," and immediately went back to sleep.

This time, there is a part of the story I've never heard. My mom said that my name made me important.

"Remember, I told you your name is royalty."

That's what she said while I was still in grade school when she told me the legacy of pain and pride attached to my name. It's also the day I became proud to carry it.

Georgia Elizabeth.

It has history – some of which is very sad.

I always knew I was named after my grandmother, Georgia Mae, and my great grandmother, Liz, but I never knew why. I learned the origin of my name in the third grade.

Liz apparently was a firecracker, and the apple didn't fall too far from the tree. From what I hear, Liz was the original Madea: a gun-carrying, cigarette-smoking, cussin', fussin' lady. She was the type of woman to fight back against wrongdoing.

And, Georgia? She was tough. She was also a community leader before people were doing it for the 'Gram. No likes. No shares. No comments. Just change. She never held a title, but she was known as a pillar of the community.

She would talk young people into turning their lives around before they crashed and burned while speeding in the wrong direction.

"Baby, why don't you get out of here and join the Army?"

Mama said she also helped feed families through her restaurant. My grandma was a hustler. I'm not sure it was all legal, but hey, get it how you live Granny!

It's a shame that I will never hear their voices. I think I am connected to those brave, inspiring women by more than a name. We are connected by spirit.

Georgia Mae Toney was murdered on Mother's Day in 1982 – five years before I was born.

She was killed by an aunt's husband after a high-speed chase. My aunt was fleeing an abusive relationship. According to court documents, the man hired someone to drive while he shot into the car. Inside the car was my grandmother, my very scared aunt and two children. My brother was just shy of 2 and my cousin was just 3 months old. A bullet grazed my brother's chest. My aunt had her arms and face blown open by the sawed-off shotgun.

My grandmother was shot, execution style, after this man forced her out of the car.

He was on the run for three months before turning himself in. Mama said he originally planned to kill the whole family, but the person he hired couldn't go through with it. He was going to blow up the family house with everyone inside. He's now serving multiple life sentences, but there is no justice for snatching a mother away from her children. I have never known my aunt without her scars. I can only imagine the nightmares she has about that day — but I've never had the nerve to ask her what happened. That's not a moment I would ever ask anyone to relive. My family is still trying to heal from it.

One day, when I was a toddler, my mom took me to the graveyard for our Mother's Day tradition. Ever since the murder, my mom and her sisters would gather to prune the weeds from the plot and place new flowers.

It was in the middle of this process that I crawled onto the tombstone and laid down with my face touching the ground. My brother said I was 3 years old when this happened. Mama said that's when she freaked out. She packed everything up and we left.

That's what I mean about having a connection to these women.

"Look at Georgia, always gotta one-up somebody," my brother will joke, 27 years later. "We put flowers down and she gon' come lay on the grave."

It isn't the only story told about me before I started school. The blessing of family is the memories they help you hold, specifically ones you were too young to keep for yourself.

Everyone tells me that young Georgia was a piece of work. She was violent and unhappy. In most of my childhood pictures, you can spot me in the corner with the balled-up face. That's what my mama calls it when my face is scrunched, my eyes are scowling, and my lips are poking out. I was so angry, and I was always looking for a fight.

But I didn't start out that way. Mama said I used to carry a purse and Bible at 2 years old and take my seat on the front row at church. I was too "saved" even before I could talk. I think mama knew something about me then. She knew I was different.

It's just taken me, like many of us, a little longer to understand what that means. The first Black president of South Africa, Nelson Mandela, explained it eloquently when he wrote.

> *"Our deepest fear is not that we are inadequate. Our deepest fear is that we are powerful beyond measure. It is our light, not our darkness, that most frightens us. We ask ourselves, 'Who am I to be brilliant, gorgeous, talented, fabulous?' Actually, who are you not to be? You are a child of God. Your playing small doesn't serve the world. There's nothing enlightened about shrinking so that other people won't feel insecure around you. We are all meant to shine, as children do. We were born to make manifest the glory of God that is within us. It's not just in some of us; it's in everyone. And as we let our own light shine, we unconsciously give other people permission to do the same. As we're liberated from our own fear, our presence automatically liberates others."*

I am Georgia Elizabeth Dawkins, which is not a name of which I was always proud. Growing up, I was ashamed. I used to dread roll call fearing that someone would make a corny ass joke about my mama being "Alabama" or being in two places at one time.

Is Alabama here? Ya mama!

Yes. My mama, and grandma, and great grandmama get tribute every time someone says my name.

I am liberated to love my name, because I know not only what it means, but how it came to be attached to me. Of course, that isn't always how I felt. I mean c'mon. I started school with a name most people associated with a state or a song.

"I bet people sing to you all the time . . ."

Seriously? How'd you guess.

As I started to learn more about my grandmother and her heart, I learned to embrace the name given to me. Ray Charles' "Georgia On My Mind" no longer sounds like torture. It is finally music to my ears.

Purpose Reflections

1. What does your name say about your purpose?

_____

_____

_____

_____

_____

_____

_____

_____

_____

_____

_____

_____

_____

_____

_____

_____

_____

_____

_____

_____

_____

_____

_____

2. How has your family influenced your purpose?

_____

_____

_____

_____

_____

_____

_____

_____

_____

_____

_____

_____

_____

_____

_____

_____

_____

_____

_____

_____

_____

_____

_____

_____

_____

– 2 –
FAMILY AND FRIENDS

I hate loud noises. I have my parents to thank for that.

At age 5 or 6, I experienced a sexual trauma that would have crumpled most people. I'll explain that later. Now, I want to tell you about the time, about the same age, I pulled a knife on my father.

He was beating my Mom like he didn't see me there. I grabbed the knife. It wasn't about hurting my father. It was about protecting my mother. Seeing him punch, kick, even whip her was not a strange sight. He'd done this for years, but this time I got in on the action. He saw the knife, and all I remember after that was falling into the aluminum closet doors.

They had been together for 13 years and had two kids, but never as husband and wife. After all of this, they then had the nerve to get married.

Seriously?

They had an actual ceremony where my mom wore a red dress. They dropped me and my brother off at a sitter and drove to the church so that the pastor could marry them. My mama claims she never even changed her name because she knew it wouldn't last — and it didn't.

They were only married three months. Then, she finally kicked him out. In a type of acceptance only a child can have, I knew it was a good thing. At 7 years old, I realized that my parents splitting up was the best decision they'd made since making me. They're both crazy on their own, but they're really insane when they're together.

I guess it was too dangerous for my father to come around after the breakup. He only sent letters for a few years. They were addressed to my brother or me and they came on holidays and birthdays, but not every holiday and not every birthday. Nevertheless, when they did come, no one could tell us that our daddy didn't love us and no one could tell us that that $10 apiece wasn't the most money in the world. Those cards, letters, and cash dulled my anger against him, as did something else.

I was in the first grade when they divorced, and I had no idea the effects the demise of their marriage had on me. To others it was obvious. My school had me in some sort of counseling program. I was getting cupcakes and prizes every Friday for years before I ever realized what it was. I thought I was in the gifted program. They were the only kids who I witnessed getting special treatment at school.

By third grade, I decided to forgive my father. I had that stirring in my spirit that I now recognize as God speaking to me. He said, "You can't hate him forever." As I write these words, I can today call him a friend.

When my dad left, my brother Ahmad became the man of the house, but he was just a kid himself. He couldn't protect me all the time. We'd just moved into our new house and my brother was in the shower. I was only 6. His friend was keeping an eye on me until he came out.

"You're my little girlfriend, right?" he asked as he laid me down on the side of the bed. "You love me, right?"

I nodded. Then he slid up my nightgown and spread my legs.

"Does that hurt?"

"No."

He couldn't go all the way. I was too tight and untouched.

I don't remember any pain.

66

**DON'T WAVER
IN YOUR FAITH
BECAUSE OF HOW
THEY REACTED TO YOUR
OBEDIENCE.**

– GEORGIA DAWKINS –

EVERYBODY
KNOWS:
THE POWER OF BEING IN POSITION

I do remember that his raping me remained our little secret until I was 17. By that time, he was already in jail for a different crime. Thank God!

The night I told my brother, he left in a rage. I'd never seen his eyes so red. I didn't want to hurt anybody, but I also didn't want my brother to find out from anyone else. My brother's feelings were precious to me and probably one of the reasons I never said anything.

Purpose Reflections

1. Are family secrets keeping you from your next level?

_____
_____
_____
_____
_____
_____
_____
_____
_____
_____
_____
_____
_____
_____
_____
_____
_____
_____
_____
_____
_____
_____

2. What are some things you have to overcome in order to get into position?

_____

_____

_____

_____

_____

_____

_____

_____

_____

_____

_____

_____

_____

_____

_____

_____

_____

_____

_____

_____

_____

_____

3. Who do you need to forgive in order to properly position yourself?

_____
_____
_____
_____
_____
_____
_____
_____
_____
_____
_____
_____
_____
_____
_____
_____
_____
_____
_____
_____
_____
_____
_____
_____
_____

– 3 –

THE END OF BLACK BOY JOY

My entire outlook on life changed when I was 11 years old thanks to the police department of Fort Myers, Florida. Granted, members of my family put me in a life-threatening position, but none of us knew that until a SWAT cop put a gun to my head. That was bad for me.

Something worse, though, happened to my little brother. It was 1998, and I was spending a few days in Fort Myers with family. My cousin and his mom were there, too. We'd mostly fill our days trying to make new friends in the neighborhood. We'd play house, hide and seek, and tag.

Most of us were at the age where you were horny, but chaste. At least, everybody else was. I guess. But at the end of the day, someone was always trying to grind up on someone else. Where I'm from, we call that hunching. There were a few boys I liked around there, but there were a few girls, too. No matter what, we always seemed to get interrupted by the piercing voice of someone's mama or the luring, melodic tune of the ice cream truck. The first three bars were like an alarm signaling that we had to find money and find it fast.

We had a routine. First, we'd pat our pockets and check our socks. If I came up short, I'd run to my aunt or even ask someone else's auntie, mama, or grandma. I'd do whatever it took to get a king-size Drumstick or my ultimate favorite, The Flip. That's what people in Southwest Florida called the solid deliciousness I know as the Snowball. These things can come in a variety of flavors: pineapple, red, grape or half-and-half. I was mostly a pineapple girl, but I also liked for my red to turn into

"

GOD PLANTED THAT SEED INSIDE
YOU BECAUSE HE KNEW YOU
COULD CARRY IT.
HE PREPARED YOU TO
DELIVER PURPOSE.
THAT GIFT IS JUST FOR YOU.

– GEORGIA DAWKINS –

EVERYBODY
KNOWS:
THE POWER OF BEING IN POSITION

pineapple. I used to lick off the glazed sugar which topped the frozen dessert and eat it with a spoon, but by this time I was a professional who licked off the glaze before rolling the cup between my hands just to flip it and eat it from the bottom. Nothing said summer in Florida like a Flip.

If I had known the childhood joy of my ice cream-eating innocence was going to end abruptly, I might have slurped down a few more.

One day, our summer memories of sugar and raging hormones were interrupted by a loud knock at the door. Then, almost immediately, someone kicked it down. I took off through the kitchen out the back door before I could see who it was. I was half way through the woods behind the house when I remembered that I'd left my little brother behind. I ran back to get him just as fast as I'd taken off, but a man from the SWAT team stopped me in my tracks.

"GET DOWN! GET DOWN!," he shouted as he pushed me to the ground. "GET ON THE FLOOR! PUT YOUR HANDS BEHIND YOUR BACK! NOW! NOW!"

I didn't know what I had done wrong. I just followed his orders. There were other men searching rooms around the house. The adults were cuffed in the living room, but they all started shouting at the SWAT cop, "You have to let her go! She's a child. She's just a child."

The SWAT officer had used twisty ties to pin my arms behind my back. It hurt. What hurt more was seeing my little brother. The right side of my face was smushed into the ground and the sight of me hog-tied with a gun to my head had him screaming as he stood next to a police car about 30 feet away.

"LET MY SISTER GO! LET MY SISTER GO!"

His eyes were no longer visible. I could only see tears and the back of his throat as he screamed with every ounce of strength he had. I could only imagine the thoughts that went through his 6-year-old brain, as he watched the masked man threaten to shoot if I moved.

Later, I found out it was a drug raid. But we were kids. We had no idea what was going on.

In the midst of the chaos, my aunt yelled, "She's only 11!" The adrenaline rush of the man with the gun to my head dropped enough to see he was pointing his weapon at a middle-school aged child. Then, he cut the plastic ties off my wrists and let me out of the house. I ran to my brother and held onto him. The rest of that day is a blur. I remember my mom coming to pick us up and the long, dark ride back home. Mama tried to make small talk, but I felt empty.

I've never really told anyone about the summer the police put a gun to my head because I was afraid of who it might hurt. That moment has emotionally scared me forever and I'm done sacrificing my healing for another person's feelings. I just hate when the truth hurts family.

I have never recovered from that day. It was also the day my brother lost every ounce of his black boy joy.

We were both just kids waiting on the ice cream truck.

Purpose Reflections

1. How has your childhood affected where you are today?

_____

_____

_____

_____

_____

_____

_____

_____

_____

_____

_____

_____

_____

_____

_____

_____

_____

_____

_____

_____

_____

_____

2. Does trauma shape your purpose or shift your purpose?

_____
_____
_____
_____
_____
_____
_____
_____
_____
_____
_____
_____
_____
_____
_____
_____
_____
_____
_____
_____
_____
_____
_____
_____
_____

– 4 –

MIDDLE SCHOOL DAZED

I was a smart kid. But because of my life experience, I filtered information a little differently than most. In retrospect, that was understandable. By age 11, I probably suffered from PTSD.

Once upon a time, I was known for my quick temper. In kindergarten, my mama beat the black off of me after I bit a white girl at school. The girl had taken my turn on the computer, so I thought I'd make her pay.

In the seconds immediately following my whoopin', mama said, "You can't do what they do. You are MY child."

From then on, I had to wait for someone to hit me before I hit them. This way, it looked like self-defense. It really didn't take much to rile me up.

There was a girl by the name of Jordan who could do no right. She could look at me wrong and I would pounce. I still remember the day I wrapped my hands around her throat and slammed her head against the wall. We were only in the first grade.

Why was I so angry?

In middle school, I tried to change my ways. First rule? No more fighting.

After that near-death experience with the police, I began to really see the value of my life. I definitely paid a lot more attention in Sunday School, and campus ministries made living for God easy with weekly worship sessions in the gym. There would always be music, scripture and doughnuts. Sometimes, there was even testimony service, and there was definitely an altar call. No campus worship service was complete without extending the invitation to salvation.

Growing up in the Church of God, I had my share of shameful walks to the front of the church; therefore, I didn't really see a need to take this walk yet again, especially not in front of my friends. All walks started the same: sweaty palms, pounding heartbeat, and tears. There were always tears. The tears were for the guilt.

How could God love me when I was so bad? What was there about me to love?

One day, we got booted from the gym due to a conflicting activity, so we had to host Campus Life outside on the basketball court. There were more than two dozen kids swinging around poles when Scott, the youth pastor, asked us to join hands. Everything stopped.

"If there is anyone here who doesn't know Jesus as their Lord and personal Savior, let them step forth . . ."

He went on and on encouraging us kids not to be afraid. I'd already completed the prayer in my head when I got "that feeling."

Sweaty palms and heart throbs, but no tears – this walk was not like the others. This walk carried purpose. We were holding hands. I dropped the hand to my left and my right and then I walked toward the middle of the circle where Scott stood. He acknowledged my brave steps and then more kids followed.

That was one of the scariest moments of my life.

What if I didn't take those steps?

What if I ignored the voice of God?

What if I continued to take for granted His grace and mercy?

Would the others have taken their steps?

It was the beginning of the school year so it wasn't too late to change my life. No one really knew me, yet. There were a few kids from my elementary school, but I assumed they were down for the ride.

But even after that, middle school was weird and my anger still controlled me at times I didn't want it to.

By the end of the school year, my grades were high – and so was my attitude. Being a minority made me very marketable when it came to education. At 12 years old, I became the recipient of a four-year academic scholarship, which was good for any public institution in Florida. The scholarship also came with a mentor to make sure I stayed on track. This was perfect because I already knew what I wanted to do. I knew I wanted to be a writer and graduate from Florida Agricultural & Mechanical University (FAMU), just like my uncle Leotis.

My uncle was a Vietnam veteran, an educator, and a lover of jazz. Mama used to drop me off at his house before she went to work. Then, I would ride to South Florida Community College with him. Riding with him was an adventure. It was only a 10-minute ride, but we made the most of it. My favorite days were the days we had to stop for gas because that meant we got to spend a little more time together. His radio dial was always placed on Tampa Bay's smooth jazz station. Sometimes we'd talk about which classes I was taking and other days we wouldn't talk at all. Either way, I looked forward to those rides.

When we got to campus, we would go our separate ways. He would go to his office and I would meet up with the College Reach Out Program (CROP). This program gave me a boost of confidence. There were both middle and high school students in the program from all over the county. We prepped for standardized tests including the ACT and SAT well before we were of age to take them. The instructors wanted us to be prepared. As little brown faces, this was necessary. A handful of the other kids also had scholarships. This helped keep us focused.

The program also included field trips like the one to a Florida Christian college. Unfortunately, there's only one thing I remember about that trip. There was a group of girls from Brooksville. They were a little older and they

“

GOD IS SO PETTY THAT HE PREPARED A WHOLE FEAST JUST FOR ME IN THE PRESENCE OF MY ENEMIES. THE FUNNY PART IS SOME PEOPLE WON'T EVEN KNOW THAT THEY'RE ENEMIES UNTIL WE RUN OUT OF FOOD.

– GEORGIA DAWKINS –

EVERYBODY
KNOWS:
THE POWER OF BEING IN POSITION

didn't seem to like me. We were staying in the dorms on campus when I heard one of the girls talking about me to a girl from back home.

Why is she letting her say those things about me?
I could hear her saying "she talks white" and "she thinks she's better than everyone else." Little did she know I had only recently been delivered.

"Do you have something you want to say?" I asked as I walked up to her in the hallway.

She then backed me into a room and started swinging. Suddenly, my fighting hands came back to me and I too began throwing punches. That's when three other girls from her group swarmed in and started punching me, too. I intended to take them all on when someone broke up the fight.

I got jumped.

I felt so alone, and I wondered why the girls from my town didn't think to take up for me. My trip was cut short. Fortunately, I got to keep my scholarship, however, they did not.

Later that summer, I found myself in another fight and this time, I was hungry for blood. My mama was in Jamaica and we were home alone. My older cousin was supposed to be watching us, but I knew that was a lie when he said it. I've never known him to stay in the same place for a long time. I was at the house playing with my younger cousin Kourtney when my little brother came home crying.

"He hit me!" he murmured through bubbles of snot and streams of tears.

"Who?" I asked before I set out to find them.

"Lynn!" He answered. "He was throwing rocks at me while I was riding my bike!"

Now y'all know how I feel about my brother. I was like a cheetah racing to hunt my prey.

"You like picking on little kids?" I said to the boy who was nearly a foot taller than I was.

I walked up to Lynn and confronted him. He didn't seem remorseful at all, and that was definitely pissing me off.

He laughed.

That's when I stepped to his face and politely asked, "Why don't you pick on someone your own size?" At the time, I didn't know that person would be me until he stepped an inch closer to my face. The next thing I knew, I'd cocked back and given him a right hook to the face. It must have really hurt because he then chased me down the street. Then, we stopped. We stopped one house before his front door behind some bushes. That's when he leaned down to pick up a chunk of the broken road. I started running backwards. I needed to be able to see which way the asphalt was going to make sure he didn't hit me in the head. He then launched it right into my stomach knocking all the oxygen out of my lungs.

"I'M GOING TO FUCKING KILL YOU!" I screamed.

I hobbled home as fast as I could. I went through every kitchen drawer until I found the butcher knife.

"Georgia, I don't think you should do that," said Kourtney on my way out the door. "You should put that back."

The whole neighborhood was watching.

"Georgia, girl, go on back home now," said one neighbor.

Then another said, "I'm a call ya mama!"

"Call her!" I said as I sped back to his house. He was still standing there.

Idiot.

He thought his mama would protect him, but I cussed her out, too.

I dared him to run up, but he didn't have the guts.

"You gon' hit me with a brick and now you scared?" I said tauntingly.

This could have gone on all day, but my aunt Teedy drove up and told me to get in the car. Lynn was lucky that day.

"Y'all, get some clothes," Aunt Teedy told us, then she took the three of us back to her house for the night.

I didn't tell her about my bruises. I saw them after my shower. My belly was all cut up, but I didn't show anyone. I was embarrassed.

When my mama got back, she was more concerned with all the cussing I did than the fighting.

I guess it was my language that made me look unruly.

I knew better, and it haunted me everywhere I went. The guilt began to weigh me down, so I went back to his house, but this time I looked for his mom, and she accepted my apology.

I never told mama about the scars on my belly.

That was a wild summer. I was two years into middle school and couldn't believe that I had stayed out of trouble. As far as the school knew, I was the golden child. My grades were good, I sang in choir, cheered, played volleyball and served as class representative. Then one day, my extracurricular activities caught up with my academics.

It was eighth grade and the school year was almost over. I was called to the girl's bathroom to fix Stephanie's hair after braiding it down the day before. She said one braid was coming undone. I had no idea this was a setup. I was braiding her hair when another girl stormed into the bathroom yelling at me. Let's just call her Jessica. She claimed I'd lied on her, and I did not have time to entertain her allegations. I remember having a really bad cold that day and I probably should not have been at school, but there we were. Stephanie ran into the crowd of girls listening outside the bathroom and that's when Jessica started swinging.

Why does this always happen to me?

Every punch I threw in return was only in self-defense. Nevertheless, that was the straw that broke the camel's back. It was my third strike. I had two prior referrals: one for disrespecting a school employee, and another for stabbing a boy with a pencil. One was a misunderstanding and the other was just a scratch. I have never stabbed anyone.

It turns out Jessica was upset because I told another friend about our kiss. What scared her excited me. I couldn't hold it, but after that fight, I wish I had held that secret a little longer. She wasn't the only girl I'd kissed, but she was the only one who wanted to fight me about it.

I lost my scholarship and I was immediately kicked off every team. No more cheering. No more volleyball. No more yearbook. No more student government.

No more Georgia.

Purpose Reflections

1. What are some personality traits that could hinder you from your purpose?

_____

_____

_____

_____

_____

_____

_____

_____

_____

_____

_____

_____

_____

_____

_____

_____

_____

_____

_____

_____

_____

_____

2. How does religion or spirituality shape your purpose?

_____

_____

_____

_____

_____

_____

_____

_____

_____

_____

_____

_____

_____

_____

_____

_____

_____

_____

_____

_____

_____

_____

_____

_____

3. Who are the people in your life who help edify your gifts?

_____
_____
_____
_____
_____
_____
_____
_____
_____
_____
_____
_____
_____
_____
_____
_____
_____
_____
_____
_____
_____
_____
_____
_____
_____
_____

– 5 –

Rebuilding My Life at Age 14

I didn't know who I was without all the titles. I also didn't know who to trust. I fought hard for my scholarship.

Who am I without this scholarship? How will I get to college now?

The minute I learned that I was losing my full ride to college, I flipped out. I took the closest, sharpest object I could find and began cutting at my wrist. No one paid me any attention. No one even noticed until my teacher looked up. There was fear in her eyes. She wasn't afraid of me, but afraid of whatever had been tormenting me from within.

I was Baker Acted. That's the Florida Law that allows emergency or involuntary mental commitment. The next thing I knew, I was in the back of a deputy's squad car being taken to a place called Peace River. It was a secluded mental facility about an hour away from home. When I arrived, I had to strip. They wanted to take any string and wire they could find on my person. Then, I talked to a doctor and explained to him that I didn't want to die, I just wanted to hurt for a little while. They locked me in a room all alone. It was cold. There was only a bed and empty walls. I was just getting comfortable when they said I had a visitor.

It was my mom. She was trying to take me home, but they said I had to stay. To my surprise, she was also with my Aunt Teedy, a woman I had never seen cry until this day. They asked the same questions that the doctor asked. I gave them the same answers. Then my aunt reached across the table and grabbed my hands.

She looked me in my eyes and she said, "This too shall pass."

I had to stay in the facility for a whole 24 hours, and the experience was scarier than the sentence. I was forced to stay in the adult ward because the adolescent ward was full. The aides said it was OK, because I didn't look like a kid anyway.

There was a woman there who checked herself in. She talked to me that night through the door. Her room was right across the hall and the empty walls made it easy for our messages to land perfectly.

There was another guy who really liked to sharpen pencils. He also taught me Spanish.

Te gusta mi cabello?

Me gusto tu pelo.

That's it! I'm cured. There's no way I belong in here with the woman who checked herself in and the guy who can't stop sharpening pencils. Who would give a mentally disabled person a pencil anyway?

My mom took me home the next day, and I decided to never scare myself, or anyone else, like that again. That wasn't the last time I tried to kill myself, but it was the last time that there were witnesses.

I had one more "rite of passage" involving gossip and groping that I had to pass the summer before high school. That's when I met the woman who hurt me worse than any man who has ever violated my body. Let's call her Alex. She was a girl I knew from church, but I'd never really talked to her until my cousin started bringing her around that summer. They would come to my house and chill. One day, my mom saw her over there and warned me, "Everyone is not your friend, Georgia."

Ain't that the truth.

Mama had to know that I wasn't trying to be friends with her like that. Alex was 19 and already a high school graduate. Mama knew that this girl was gay, and she also knew that everyone else knew she was gay. It wasn't about the basketball shorts she wore two sizes too big, nor was it about the two sports bras she wore to keep her breasts strapped down. It was about the energy she carried and her arrogance. What was intriguing to me caused mama to worry.

Sometimes she'd bring food for my brother and me. I was always babysitting, and that's why she brought along my cousin. Because there was someone there to watch him, she could get me alone. One day she gave me her keys and told me I could drive. I was 14 and I had never driven a car before. At first, my cousin and my brother rode with us, but when I almost hit a mailbox, they opted to get out and walk.

I wanted to walk, too. I wanted to drive, but I didn't want it like this. My being vulnerable allowed her to be extra helpful, which required a lot more touching than your typical Drivers Ed course.

When we got back to the house, we went into my room and closed the door.

"Are you ready?" she asked.

"I think so." I replied trembling.

It was the first time I had given anyone permission to touch me. It wasn't at all like the games of tag that led to dry humping and playing house. This was different. It didn't feel right, and it didn't feel wrong. I was confused. I was confused about what I was giving her permission to do. I thought we were playing another game of "I'll touch yours if you touch mine," only she wouldn't let me touch her. She tried to excite me but I stopped her. I was terrified. This was as far as I had ever gone.

A few days later, I found out that I was just another girl for her to brag about. I had family members calling me from across town and out of state.

"Are you gay now?"

"Were you just experimenting?"

"Did she take advantage of you?"

"Nothing happened!" I told each and every person that she made the whole thing up.

It never happened.

That's what I wanted to believe. I wanted to be able to see her mom at church and not throw up in my mouth. It still amazes me to this day that no one appeared to judge her even though what she did was illegal. I was only 14, molested for a second time in my life.

My only chance to reclaim the image I wanted for myself was to start over again in high school. That's when I planned to prove to everybody that they were wrong about me.

I needed to prove to the school that I was not going to be the little Black girl causing trouble and embarrassing herself. I also needed to prove to my family and my community that I was successful. Not gay. Not angry. Not crazy. I needed to prove success. I used to tell myself that I'd come back one day with a beautiful ring, a rich man who loved me, and some kids. That was the picture of success in my eyes at that time.

That's when I started changing. I didn't really feel like I fit in with most of the Black kids, so I avoided them. Not all of them, just most of them. I ended up hanging around the cool kids and the smart kids who were most often the "Brown kids." That was our joke for the Black and Indian kids who were in the honors classes. Taking honors and Advanced Placement classes pushed me academically. This was promising for someone who needed money to go to college.

I did everything I could to stay out of trouble. I was a member of every team and nearly all organizations: the track and field team, the swim team, the weightlifting team, the varsity soccer team, varsity choir, Key Club president, Students Working Against Tobacco, and senior class vice president.

I also worked multiple jobs at a time. By the time I was 16, I worked at the movie theater, Bob Evans, Wendy's, a doctor's office, and for market researchers in the mall. We were the people who followed you from store to store to see if you wanted to take a survey. Sometimes, we even offered money. During the school year, I worked at least two jobs per week. By summer, I worked full-time at Central Florida Health Care. I was a nursing assistant. I didn't know that was a real position, until they hired me. It was my job to input the immunization records into the system. At that time, the clinic was a part of a huge digital transition.

The best part of my job at the clinic was working alongside Auntie Teedy – "Nurse Teedy," as they called her on the floor. She had her own office in the back. It was warm and cozy. The first thing I noticed was the window. I'd seen it before when my brother I came in for checkups. We'd surprise her and hang out in her office while my mama caught her up on the latest gossip. The window didn't look as big then, but I was now seeing them through the eyes of a worker and not an adolescent. Now, I better understood the value of peace and space.

There was also a bookshelf with pictures of the whole family. Each one had their own frame, which added a little personality to the shelf. Of course, there were books, too, but I can't say I ever picked one up. I loved sitting in her chair. It made me feel powerful. Auntie knew it, too, so sometimes she'd just let me sit there and spin. This was Black Girl Magic for me. Before it was a hashtag or a t-shirt slogan, it was the joy of seeing another black woman shine while whispering to yourself, "I want to be just like her one day."

Two of my favorite office accessories included her radio and the Holy Bible. The tape was always cued up to "Order My Steps" by the Brooklyn Tabernacle Choir, and the Bible was always open to Psalms 91.

Everything appeared to be going well for me in high school, but that was not the case. While I was traveling to sing or to compete for whatever sport that season, I was still struggling spiritually.

I had boyfriends, at times more than one. I even let them kiss me, but behind every saliva swap was a fantasy that didn't include the man in front of me. I can't remember a time in my life when I didn't have a crush on a girl. It's not that I didn't like guys, I just didn't like them as much.

In preparation for college, my auntie would say, "Don't go up there to FAMU and get caught up. Those men up there have nice cars, they're smart, and some of them even come from money."

"Yes, ma'am!" I replied knowing she didn't have a thing to worry about.

"We should put you on birth control," she suggested.

"I'm just going to stay focused."

I tried to pray it away. I tried to fast it away. I even tried running around the church until I could only feel the love of God. I felt Him, but I felt this, too.

When my family found out that I made the Homecoming Court, they couldn't wait to go shopping. They had me in Macy's and Dillard's. Shopping was fun then because I was my ideal size. I knew I was fine when I bought a pair of size 12 jeans from the Gap. I wore them until I grew out of them, but watching my aunties shop for me was fun.

"Go put this on," said one auntie.

"Nah, her butt too big for that," another answered.

Come on.

I've always had a big butt. My auntie claims people thought I was still in diapers at 4 years old.

> **MAKE NO MISTAKE.**
> **SOMETIMES PEOPLE KNOW**
> **EXACTLY WHO YOU ARE**
> **BUT THEY KNOW YOU DON'T KNOW**
> **WHO YOU ARE SO THEY TAKE**
> **ADVANTAGE OF THAT.**

– GEORGIA DAWKINS –

EVERYBODY
KNOWS:
THE POWER OF BEING IN POSITION

I didn't win Homecoming Queen, but it's an honor to just be nominated.

Not!

The system was rigged! There's no way I came in as the FOURTH runner up. No one understood it, especially me. I campaigned hard and everybody liked me – or so I thought.

"Georgia, everybody's not going to like you," my big brother Ahmad once said to me.

"What?" I replied in a confused tone.

I felt like he told me the sky was green and the grass was blue.

"Yeah, Georgia, some people will not like you just because they cannot like you."

I knew that everything he said was true.

My high school graduation party was a blast. My whole family came down. Our house was full of people including Richard. I'm still not completely sure if we were dating, but he definitely bought me a ring and I definitely lost it. So, I'm paranoid because I'm thinking everyone else is thinking that Richard is thinking that he's my man.

Then, my uncle walks up to me with a beer in his hand and says, "I don't know why we're throwing you a party."

"Well, I just graduated," I said.

"Yeah, that's what you're supposed to do. Why are we celebrating something that you're supposed to do anyway?"

At first, I wanted to be offended by this statement, but I was not. Graduating is not an accomplishment; it is an expectation. It was the least I could do for all those who never had the opportunity to even learn how to read.

Purpose Reflections

1. Was there ever a time where you considered taking your own life?

_____

_____

_____

_____

_____

_____

_____

_____

_____

_____

_____

_____

_____

_____

_____

_____

_____

_____

_____

_____

_____

_____

_____

2. How do you make mental health a priority in your life?

_____
_____
_____
_____
_____
_____
_____
_____
_____
_____
_____
_____
_____
_____
_____
_____
_____
_____
_____
_____
_____
_____
_____
_____

– 6 –
LOST AND LOSS

My family can take credit for some of the most traumatic moments of my life. But family members also gave me my sense of purpose.

Family is the reason I'm a journalist.

My uncle was the whole reason I wanted to go to FAMU for journalism.

When the envelope came telling me that I had been accepted, I forced a river of tears down my throat as I held the letter in my hand. Then, I picked up the phone.

"Hello!"

"Auntie, I got in," I said weeping.

"You got into FAM, huh?" I could hear her smiling through the receiver.

"Yes, ma'am."

"Georgia got in y'all!" she announced. "Yeah, she crying."

Florida A&M University was the only college I applied to, but it wasn't the only college I thought I would attend. The Internet tried to distract me with Howard University and Hampton University. I started applications to both, but never completed either one. Then, I thought I would attend Spelman College with my best friend Roxanne. The only problem was she was a year ahead of me and that gave me some time to think.

Why did I want to attend Spelman? Was it for Roxanne or how I thought it might look on a resume if I went to a private Black college?

Well, if I was going to go through all that, I should have just applied to Bethune-Cookman College (BCC at the time), and that was completely out of the question. There's a rivalry in my family between the now Bethune-Cookman University and A&M, how old school Rattlers refer to FAMU. At one point, I had an uncle and a cousin who played football for BCC, but I had way more cousins who graduated from FAMU.

Besides, the uncle I admired so much, Leotis, was a FAMU graduate. Florida A&M was it for me.

One day, while we were shopping in Tampa for dorm supplies, I saw a lady in the shoe store wearing a sorority shirt. It was pink and green just like the pictures I saw online.

She could only be wearing that if she went to college. I should bother her.

"Excuse me, miss," I said as I walked a little closer.

Not that close, maybe within five feet.

"What college did you attend?" I asked.

"I graduated from Northwestern in Chicago," she replied as she turned back to examine the shoes that caught her eye.

"What was your major?" I asked, trying to keep her engaged.

"I studied journalism and communications," she said.

What are the odds that the stranger I chose to bother in the store would be in my future field?

She went on to explain that she was a reporter for about ten years before she got out of the business.

"If you want to be a journalist, you need to join NABJ," she suggested.

The National Association of Black Journalists? Who knew we needed such a thing?

She had relocated to Tampa for a change of pace, which is what she found working in communications for the Moffitt Cancer Center. I knew all about Moffitt. That's where my cousin Dolly went for cancer treatment each of the three times she was diagnosed. My family had been through a lot in the last two years. We lost Dolly and Uncle Track to cancer, back-to-back. Uncle Track was my mom's older brother and Dolly was my mom's niece. Uncle Track, whose real name was Benjamin, was a preacher, and Dolly, also known as Henrietta, was the "saved" cousin. I looked to them both at times when I needed something to believe in. Their faith gave me hope. They were two of the people who were most proud of me, and neither one lived long enough to see me graduate from high school and move on to college.

It would have been great to have them as sounding boards when I tried to make my first friends on campus.

Unfortunately, my roommate and I got started on the wrong foot, and it was my fault. When I reached out over the summer, I tried to bond way too fast. I was used to people responding to my humor, but she was not a fan.

"You must be Baptist," I said in our first phone conversation.

"I am," she said. "Why do you ask?"

"I can hear it in your voice."

It's ironic that we were divided over denomination because I would need more faith that year than I ever needed my whole life.

After joining NABJ and volunteering for the school paper, The FAMUAN, I needed to find some balance. My friends Maui and Quaila suggested I join the FAMU Gospel Choir.

Singing? That's easy.

Little did they know; I'd just come back from touring with the Florida Ambassadors of Music for 16 days in Europe. We stopped in seven countries including England, France, Liechtenstein, Italy, Austria, Germany and Switzerland. I'd never been so far away from home. Gospel choir was not Sebring High School's Varsity Choir. I mean, there were no music sheets, but they sounded amazing.

The vibrato we demonstrated in high school may have raised a few strands of hair on a dozen arms, but the vibrato that came out of the gospel choir made people jump out of their seats.

This is not what I'm used to, but here goes.

Being in the FAMU Gospel Choir changed the way I worshipped. I grew up in a Pentecostal church, so I was convinced that I'd seen every shout and experienced every anointing. I was wrong. There's just something about getting a group of college kids together who not only want God, but desire to tell the world about Him.

Whenever I couldn't be found with the choir or hanging out in J-School, I was most likely eating in the Cafe. I was with my girls Maya and Monique — who happened to be cousins — when we caught the attention of a group of strangers. They spotted us in the center of the cafeteria and decided to approach.

Sometimes there are people who just want to dominate.

That was the case with this group of four or five "super-Christians." They had one clear leader. She was in her 30s and shared a testimony about being delivered from drugs and a fast life. She explained that God had given her a second chance, so she followed His voice and started this student-led ministry on the campus of Savannah State University. I went back to their hotel that night. There were about seven of them staying in one room, so we turned it into a sleepover. I didn't have clothes or a toothbrush. I just went because I felt comfortable.

These women ran their group like a cult. Their whole goal was to keep people out of Greek letter organizations. Oh, and save souls in the name of Jesus, but they were completely joyless. If someone complimented us on our outfit or makeup, we were not allowed to say "thank you." Showing gratitude meant we were taking credit for what God allowed us to have. Instead, we were to replace it with "Thank you, Jesus" or "Praise God!"

They taught us to find the devil in everything, including music. They told us Jay-Z was the devil because of the Roc. They told us it meant that he wanted people to worship him. They reminded us that Lucifer was once the angel of music. I remember going home that night and throwing away all of my music, my DVDs and burning my journals. Whatever reminded me of the old Georgia had to go.

By this time, I'd recruited a few friends to fill out my chapter's quota for this ministry.

Whenever the group would come in from Savannah, we'd have prayer sessions. One night, we prayed around the eternal flame on campus in the middle of the rain. The flame burns all day and all night. It commemorates the University's selection by Time Magazine as "College of the Year" in 1997. I'd be out all night praying and studying with the ministry just to have to wake up at 6 a.m. for the group prayer line.

Shortly after meeting them, they invited me to Savannah State's Homecoming. I rode there with a friend from Florida State University. When I say friend, I mean we'd met a few days prior in preparation for this trip. We both promised to be charter chapters at our schools for the ministry.

Even though they forbade us from pledging, everything about them was very Greek. We had a hand sign, group colors, a line name, a stroll and a process. The process of purity was a nearly three-day experience. It started on a Friday and ended on a Sunday. We spent at least two nights in a hotel conference room crying out to God after our sessions. We were learning doctrine for the organization. Our spiritual names came around this time as well, but there was a catch. We were to pray and ask God to reveal the name, but He would only reveal it to the

"

HEAR ME WHEN I TELL YOU,
GIRL, YOU CANNOT PUT
EVERYBODY ON.
YOU WILL DROWN TRYING TO
RESCUE THE PEOPLE WHO WERE
NEVER TAUGHT
HOW TO SWIM.

– GEORGIA DAWKINS –

EVERYBODY
KNOWS:
THE POWER OF BEING IN POSITION

leader. Our name came complete with a scripture and prophetic word. My name was Lady Proclaim.

Like I said. Cult. One person gets the message and changes your identity.

When we arrived for Homecoming weekend at their school, we received a warning instead of a welcome.

"They don't really like us here," said one girl.

"Yeah, we got suspended from campus for hazing," said another girl.

"What do they think you did?" I was slightly scared at this point, but I needed to know.

"A part of our process used to be the washing of the feet, but by definition it's hazing."

Whew! No one got hurt.

I called my mama to let her know I got to the campus safely, but she had other questions.

"Who did you say you were with?" she asked because mamas have to know everything.

I explained that I was with the ministry and I was staying at their house.

"That sounds like a group home!" she told me with her tone turning slightly more concerned.

I was so offended by her choice of words. I assumed my mama didn't know any better, but mama knows, honey. Mama always knows.

I ended up leaving that ministry after only 90 days. I drew the line when they gave me an ultimatum of them or gospel choir. Conflicting event dates, where I signed up to travel with the choir – and paid my money – were at the same time the ministry planned their event. Nevertheless, they told me I had to choose. No problem. I chose the choir. Choir was the opportunity that I prayed for from the beginning. God never told me to join that ministry. As much as I wanted it to be the right thing to do, it set me back.

Once I stepped away and stopped payment on the letterman's jacket with my spiritual name on the back, they shunned me. No one from the group was allowed to talk to me on campus. This went on for weeks until someone else decided to quit as well. My real friends apologized for treating me that way, and I had no problem forgiving them. Lost is lost.

I found out a short time later that Uncle Leotis had a cancerous brain tumor.

Immediately, I remembered him complaining about headaches months before I went off to school.

Was he sick this whole time?

Mama said they were trying to keep it from me because they wanted me to focus on school. I cried that day until I could no longer produce tears. My roommate was even concerned. She made sure I had a friend with me. She even got me a card. Jasmine came and crawled into the twin-sized bed and held me. Then we prayed. I just didn't understand why cancer would dare attack the strongest man in the world.

Gospel Choir had a performance coming up it Orlando. It was Florida Classic weekend and that meant time for the biggest rivalry in Black college football history.

The whole weekend is a big deal if you grew up black in Florida.

I was really looking forward to this year's game because it was my first game as a Rattler. All the other years, I as just a wannabe. I thought that it was finally my time but it wasn't, because my family wasn't there. I picked up an orange alumni shirt for Uncle Leotis. It reminded me of all the vintage sweaters he'd given me over the years. My favorite was "Black by Popular Demand." It's a sweater my uncle bought in the 80s that I still wear to this day.

A week after that game, my friend Nefertiti, was murdered by one of her roommates. Rumor had it that he was in love with her. I was with my aunt in Atlanta when I got the call. I wanted to honor her for all that she did to inspire me as a freshman and as an aspiring journalist. I couldn't think of a better way to do it than with words.

A newspaper publisher from back home asked me what I wanted to write about. I said college. The deal was I'd report on local events when I was in town, plus I got the chance to write a bi-weekly column called "On my Mind." Writing for *The News-Sun* made me a professional journalist before I finished my first semester of school. It was also a great way to keep in touch with my hometown.

Meeting and losing Nefertiti was the first piece I wrote. Fortunately, My uncle lived long enough to see my first published article. Then, I had to write about him.

Miracles don't always work out the way we hope. There are times when it takes all we have just to go on one more day. Life is full of surprises. Some satisfy us and some cause us to question our existence. At times we even question God's will.

When my uncle was diagnosed with cancer in November, I immediately applied my faith to the situation. I started believing God for a healing. Excitement overwhelmed me because in the back of my mind I just knew that God would bring him through. I knew He would bring us through.

Shortly after his diagnosis, I spoke with a woman who is very dear to my heart. She asked me how my family was, and I explained to her our ordeal, but I told her not to worry because I believed God for a miracle. She responded by telling me about the many people she had lost in her lifetime. She said that she had learned that a miracle is not always a healing; sometimes a miracle is being able to make it through the situation.

I must say that this is the hardest lesson I have ever had to learn. Never in my life have I prayed or fasted as I did for this "miracle." I did not know how to react when I heard the news that my uncle had died, anyway. First, I wanted to cry because I had lost him, and then I wanted to rejoice because I knew that he was no longer in pain.

To comfort myself, I began to reminisce.

The number one misconception about my relationship to Leotis is people think that he was just my uncle, but he was so much more. He was my father and a role model. He was the reason I chose to go into journalism and the reason Florida A&M was my only selection for college. My aunt and my uncle are an extra set of parents that God blessed me with. They have always been there for me and they have taught me a great deal.

At my graduation party the summer earlier, Uncle Leotis made a comment about how we should not be celebrating my graduation.

"Why are we celebrating something she is supposed to do?"

At first, I didn't quite understand, but then I realized that he was right. We spend too much time celebrating people for things they are supposed to do. Because of that, people get comfortable with what they are doing and do not desire to exceed average expectations.

Although my will was not done, I was happy to know that he was no longer suffering. I found comfort in my God, my friends, and my family. Many of my friends showed care and concern during my time of need. They knew it was hard to suffer that type of loss and not be at home.

One of my friends shared a song with me by Byron Cage titled "I Understand." It really helped me through the week. In this song, the singer tells God how he just feels like he can't go on because he is tired, and life is so hard. God responds by saying, "When you can't hear my voice, just trust my plan."

God's plan for my life was just beginning to unfold.

Purpose Reflections

1. How has heartbreak affected your relationship with yourself?

_____
_____
_____
_____
_____
_____
_____
_____
_____
_____
_____
_____
_____
_____
_____
_____
_____
_____
_____
_____
_____
_____
_____
_____

2. What is your truth?

_____
_____
_____
_____
_____
_____
_____
_____
_____
_____
_____
_____
_____
_____
_____
_____
_____
_____
_____
_____
_____
_____
_____
_____
_____

3. What are you most afraid of when it comes to living your truth?

_____

_____

_____

_____

_____

_____

_____

_____

_____

_____

_____

_____

_____

_____

_____

_____

_____

_____

_____

_____

_____

_____

_____

_____

– 7 –

'OUT' of College: On to a Career

The following year, I took on even more responsibilities.

I was now an editor for The FAMUAN and president of the FAMU Association of Black Journalists. I was also carrying a 16-hour course load and working two jobs. I thought I could do it all, until I became very depressed. I stopped putting any effort into my appearance, which thankfully has been documented by Facebook. When I look back on those pictures, it makes me so sad because I remember that valley. I remember staying up all night at rehearsal just to come home and work on an article for the paper and plan for the chapter. It all became too much.

A friend suggested I go see one of the counselors on campus. I refused.

"I've been praying about it. This too shall pass," I said, quoting the words my Aunt Teedy once spoke to comfort me.

I felt like I was spending more time crying than actually studying. The depression became a huge distraction and my grades were suffering. The thought of my grades falling and losing my scholarships as a result was terrifying.

If I fail, I have to go back home.

That friend finally convinced me to make the call. I cried my eyes out that first session. Our conversation revealed that I was struggling with more than just the stress of school and pride, but sexuality. This man actually

> ## SOMETIMES BEING IN GOD'S WILL MEANS YOU DON'T GET THE CREDIT. YOU HAVE TO BE OK WITH YOUR NAME NOT BEING ON THE GROUP PROJECT.

– GEORGIA DAWKINS –

EVERYBODY
KNOWS:
THE POWER OF BEING IN POSITION

said to me, "I think you are gay and that you are in love with her."

Who hired this guy?

He was suggesting that I was in love with one of my closest friends – the same friend who convinced me to go to therapy. I was shocked at first, but then I was relieved. His expert opinion meant that all those feelings were not in my head. I took it as, "You're not crazy. You just have a broken heart."

I decided to share these new revelations with the person who urged me to find out about myself in the first place. My voice was shaking. I didn't know how to tell her what the doctor had just told me. She was getting on a flight and I didn't want to start such a sensitive topic if we really didn't have the time to flesh it out.

She forced my lips to say, "He thinks I'm in love with you."

"Oh, I can see that," she replied.

ARE YOU KIDDING ME? You mean she knew I was in love with her this whole time, and she just let me suffer in silence?

When I came out two years later, she said we could not be friends again until I got married or delivered. She called it my "issue," as if I were bleeding my life away and just needed to touch the hem of His garment. After that, she disappeared for five months. She reappeared for five years before vanishing again. Her disappearing act nearly shattered my heart, but I knew it was for the best.

I went on with my life and prayed for the next step in my career and was still completely surprised when it hit me in the face.

ABC News called.

A cheery voice on the other end of the phone claimed I'd applied for some sort of diversity fellowship. I didn't remember anything about it, but I just went with it. She said they wanted to set up an interview, so I agreed.

"Thursday, 10 a.m. Got it!"

I hung up and ran to my computer.

It was 2008, and I was just a sophomore. After my unpaid internship in Orlando, I promised myself I would never do another unpaid internship. It's not that I thought I was "too good." It's just that I knew my worth. My 10-week stint in Orlando was painful, yet, rewarding. I knew I had to make a sacrifice for the experience. It came at a cost. Sebring, Florida didn't have a TV station. I had to commute. I drove an hour-and-a-half on Sundays to work at the station eight hours a day on Monday and Tuesday. Tuesday night I drove back to Sebring and worked at the clinic Wednesday through Friday as the assistant to the nursing staff. It was a lot! But it helped me prove to myself what I was made of. Still, I'm not doing all that for little or nothing again.

After that experience, I started applying for any and every opportunity that would let me. I even applied for film internships in Los Angeles. I was willing to do anything, but be broke.

According to Gmail, on March 10, 2008, I applied for the ABC News UNITY Digital Fellowship.

"ABC NEWS is seeking candidates to participate in a groundbreaking fellowship opportunity."

This sounds familiar.

"Candidates should be junior, senior, or graduate level students."

Why the hell did I apply for this? I was only a sophomore. A very bold and ambitious sophomore.

Hey Thursday! So, the lady calls me and I'm nervous as all get out. She asks me a series of questions about current events and I ace them! Clearly, I'm still a student and I'm tested on these topics daily. Then, the questions get a little more difficult. She starts asking about situations where I had been a leader.

Next, she asked me about diversity. I remember saying something like, "I don't respect news organizations that don't have diversity behind the camera. Blah blah. I want to work with people who look like me. Blah blah." It was very militant and very BLACK! I knew immediately they would not waste time offering me a job. Still, I spent weeks pacing the floor and talking myself out of emailing the recruiter.

Two weeks later, the e-mail came.

DEAR FELLOW CANDIDATE:

I am pleased to congratulate you on being selected to participate in the ABC NEWS/UNITY DIGITAL FELLOWSHIP this summer.

I slid out of my chair and began sobbing in my hands. It was like the day I got into FAM but better. I'd never felt so undeserving of an honor like this.

I thought to myself, *this is what favor feels like.*

Those were not my thoughts when I looked for a place to live. Finding housing in New York City was impossible. I would stay up all night searching for a room with no budget. I put out calls on Craigslist, MySpace, and Facebook. Then, I lucked up. I found a room on 94th and Columbus for $650 per month. I didn't have all the money, but my dean pitched in.

Dr. James Hawkins was like having another father figure in my life. He was everything I loved about my Uncle Leotis and everything I thought my father could be. He looked out for me. That summer, he not only found money for me to secure housing, but he allowed me to store my personal items inside the school. I'm talking my microwave, ironing board, and winter clothes were all scattered around the School of Journalism and Graphic Communication. Some students thought I was spoiled.

Others even thought I was his daughter because our last names sound so much alike. While there was absolutely no relation, Dean Hawkins saw me for who I could be, and he always made sure my dreams came true.

That summer at ABC was both the most rewarding and traumatic experience of my life. One day, I had the most-read story on ABCNews.com, and the next day I'm feeling like I failed. Or, I could have just filmed and edited video for *World News Tonight with Charles Gibson* and someone tell me that I thought I was better than everyone else and crush my spirit. I was up and down all the time. I didn't know who to trust or what to believe. Everyone around me was giving me pats on the back and saying I'd did a great job, but my supervisor said I should ask fewer questions and listen more.

Budding journalists shouldn't ask a lot of question. Got it.

Purpose Reflections

1. Who inspires you?

_____

_____

_____

_____

_____

_____

_____

_____

_____

_____

_____

_____

_____

_____

_____

_____

_____

_____

_____

_____

_____

_____

_____

_____

_____

2. Who stirs up the gifts inside of you?

_____
_____
_____
_____
_____
_____
_____
_____
_____
_____
_____
_____
_____
_____
_____
_____
_____
_____
_____
_____
_____
_____
_____
_____
_____

3. How do you encourage purpose in others?

_____
_____
_____
_____
_____
_____
_____
_____
_____
_____
_____
_____
_____
_____
_____
_____
_____
_____
_____
_____
_____
_____
_____
_____
_____

– 8 –

Paying My Dues

Great! Now there's one more person I have to prove wrong.

One day she asked me about talking to ABC news anchor Robin Roberts on the street. The supervisor made it sound like I was stalking Robin. I had to explain to her that Robin and I were both returning to the building when I simply stopped to shake her hand. What my supervisor didn't know was Robin and I had a mutual friend who went to FAMU. When she found out I knew her mentee, she invited me up to her office.

Tears started to flow almost immediately after I sat down. I explained to Ms. Roberts that I'd recently lost my uncle to cancer and seeing her brought back a lot of memories. I went on and on about how he was the whole reason I got into journalism. She handed me a tissue and told me it was going to be OK.

"He's proud of you," she said.

I dried my eyes.

"What do you want to do?" I couldn't believe that one of the most talented journalists in the world was interviewing me.

"I don't want to be a talking head."

Dammit! That slipped out before I had time to filter it.

"It's OK." Robin said while nodding in agreement. "I know what you mean."

"I mean I want to be a producer."

What happened next shows the power of divine order and how tightly knit the broadcast community's referral system can be. Not only did Robin ask me follow up questions, but she began putting me in touch with other Black female producers including her own, Quiana, who treated me like her little sister. I also learned that my supervisor had been an incredible senior producer before she became a recruiter.

Aha!

I spent the next five weeks volunteering for everything. If my supervisor needed something transcribed, I was there. If her assistant had to step out, I was there. If she needed lunch, I was there. I knew I was not an intern, but I also believed in being humble. This woman may have looked like me, but she did not know me. How she felt about my perception had nothing to do with my performance. It's all a game.

I was there to play.

During our final lunch of the summer, I reminded my supervisor about the uncomfortable conversation we had just a few weeks prior.

"How would you grade my performance now?" I asked before swallowing my fear.

"Let's just say, if this were summer camp, you would get the most improved award."

That was all I needed to hear. ABC News brought me back for two summers after that. This time, I was neither intern nor a fellow. I was a desk assistant. That's an entry-level role! They gave me an entry-level role before I even graduated.

Who does that? God. God does that.

During my last summer, Auntie Robin, as I now called her, would give me little pep talks along the way. I remember walking the halls of the Times Square studio trying to pretend I was anywhere but there. It's not that the opportunity wasn't great. I was just really over people. I was training this girl who really hated me at the time.

Another sister.

"

I WAS ALWAYS THERE FOR YOU
EXCEPT FOR THE DAY
THAT I HAD TO SHOW UP
FOR MYSELF.

– GEORGIA DAWKINS –

EVERYBODY
KNOWS:
THE POWER OF BEING IN POSITION

I couldn't figure out why she disliked me, when all I ever tried to do was help her. Some people don't deserve your kindness. That's a lesson I've had to learn the hard way. So, I'm walking and trying to figure out world peace when I hear whistling. The tune to "Georgia on my Mind" stopped me in my tracks. I turned around and saw that it was Auntie Robin. I was blessed to see her before the rest of the world even heard her voice. No makeup. No labels. No heels. Just freckles. Just joy. In one motion, she grabbed the nape of my neck and kissed my forehead.

She said, "Whatever it is, it's going to be alright."

She was my auntie whether she wanted to be or not. She just fit the description. One day she invited me to ride with her and Quiana back to our offices on 66th street. I normally took the train, but I was not about to tell Robin, "No." I jumped in.

"What are you going to do next?" Robin asked as Quiana scrolled through email.

I was looking to Quiana for direction. I needed her to interpret which Robin I was getting. I was able to deduce that this was a cross between "Auntie Robin" and "For Good Morning America, I'm Robin Roberts."

"I don't know. I think I'll just come back here." I tried telling her what I thought she wanted to hear. "They want me to come back."

"That's great, but what do you really want to do?" she pressed on.

She may as well have been holding a spotlight to my face in the heat of an interrogation room. I was sweating. I only had four months of school left. Then what?

"I want to produce at network."

"Good. Good. That's good." It's like she knew what I was going to say before the words escaped my mouth.

"Some of the best producers at the network came from local news."

Is this really happening? Is Robin Roberts really giving me career advice in the back of her town car? This can't be real.

"If you want to make it here, you have to go. Go local! Grow fast and grow strong then come back."

With Robin's blessing, I did almost exactly what she said. I went back to local news, but I sold myself short. I returned to Tallahassee to finish school in August of 2010. I immediately applied to WCTV. It was the leading news outlet in the area. Almost everyone who was serious worked at WCTV or WTXL. WTXL was the ABC affiliate, but WCTV was the dominant station. I applied to be an intern, but the news director called to say I didn't get it.

"Georgia, I'm afraid you're overqualified," said Triston Sanders, who was also the evening anchor at the station. Everyone knew who she was.

"Listen, I have an opening for a Daybreak producer. Would you be interested in that?" she asked. I started the job two weeks later.

Uh oh! It's happening. I might be doing too much again.

The dean had just given me an override to take 17 hours that semester. It was almost 19, but I scaled it back. He didn't seem completely confident in my performance when he signed the paper, but he knew I was crazy enough to pull it off. So, I'm taking a million classes, working a part-time job overnight and working in the dean's office four days a week. I was also a member of the NABJ board of directors. I was elected by the student membership in 2009 and it was a huge responsibility. It was a two-year commitment and I could see the finish line.

Carrying such a heavy load meant I had to sacrifice a lot of the fun stuff. If the party wasn't at my house, I wasn't going. There was hardly any time to party when there was always an assignment due for class, a report due for NABJ, or I was due at work.

For four months, I slept in my car. After I got off at 6 a.m., I'd pull up to campus, turn up the heat, lock my doors and crawl in the backseat for a little nap. I just wanted to be on time. I needed to prove to everyone who believed in me that I could pull it off. And, I did.

By the end of the semester, I had a job offer to be a producer in Fort Myers, Florida.

Well, I knew where that was.

This was perfect. It was full-time with benefits and only 90 minutes away from home. This was the first time that I'd lived somewhere where my name was the only name on the lease. My mama delivered my bed from home. Then, my auntie bought me a couch from a garage sale, and another gave me a dining room table and pillows to match the sofa. I was living the life until I had to do math. I was not making enough money to survive. Eventually, I had to get a second job. I started teaching media to the kids at the Quality Life Center where I volunteered. For months, I worked 7 days a week. The five days I worked at the TV station overlapped with the five days I worked with the kids. Those tiny people kept me grounded. I was there to help them, but they helped me more than I knew. It wasn't about the money. It was about my purpose.

In 2012, I was given the Southwest Florida 40-under-40 Award by Gulfshore Business Magazine. It's an award given to rising stars in the community, but I knew my time in Fort Myers was coming to an end. The tide was changing at work and I had to move out and move fast.

A few months before my contract was set to end, I moved out of my apartment and moved in with my friend Barry. The move was supposed to save me money, and after my car broke down staying with him saved me hundreds. You see, Barry lived across the street from the TV station, but I would still drive just to be extra safe rolling up at midnight. I was two months out from the end of my contract when my car shut off in the middle of the parking lot.

While it was rolling away, I shifted the gear into neutral and pushed it back into the parking space, all while wearing a dress. I was a little late to work that day, but my circumstance only made me want to fight harder. I needed to get out of there. For one, I needed more money, and two, I was miserable. There was no room for me to grow after two years with the company.

In 2013, I got out of my contract and moved to Shreveport, Louisiana. I was hired as senior producer. I didn't know a soul, but I knew a lot of people who knew people who knew some more people. I had to buy a new car just to drive 16 hours to North Louisiana. I ended up crashing on a couch that belonged to a friend of a friend and that friend just happened to live with his mom and his sister.

Beggars can't be choosers!

When I wasn't staying there, I lived with Shakari, a young journalist who worked at The Shreveport Times. I met her through a FAMU alumna. Shakari graduated from Grambling State University, but I didn't hold that against her. Our HBCU rivalry was one of the things that bonded us.

After two years in Port City, I knew it was time to move on. Hell, 18 months in I was already applying for the next job, and when I wasn't applying for jobs, I was applying for fellowships. I got two in the same year. The Society of Professional Journalists (SPJ) selected me as one of six Diversity Leadership Fellows. A month later, the Journalism and Women Symposium (JAWS) named me one of 10 Emerging Journalists. These conferences saved my life. I was on the brink of a depression stemming from frustration at work. Professional development conferences helped me shape my plan.

The next thing I knew, I was headed to graduate school in New York City. My interview with the City University of New York (CUNY) felt good. I knew my references were great, but I didn't really expect to get in. Still, I made a big announcement and sprinkled a little glitter on my resignation letter. My friend Felecia even threw me a going away party. Dozens of people showed up to celebrate. I was overwhelmed.

My heart was extra full around this time because I had reunited with an old flame. Makayla and I had dated three years prior, but things didn't work out for us. I wore the blame for many years because I was in between breakups during the time we met. This time, we were both single again and looking forward to our second chance.

During our road trip to Sebring, Florida, I got an email and pulled over on the side of the road. We were on I-49 headed to New Orleans for the night. The email was from CUNY.

I didn't get the scholarship.

I was devastated. There was no way I could go back to New York City and be poor. I didn't live like a student the first three times I lived there so why regress?

In the remaining hours of our road trip, I talked myself out of the entire degree and decided to get a job. I stayed with my mom in Sebring and flew all over the country for interviews. From Chicago to Charlotte, I was keeping my options open. Impatient and frustrated, I decided to take a job in Tampa with the station I grew up watching. My family was finally able to watch a newscast I produced without going online.

Makayla decided to take a job in Tampa, too. Neither one of us was interested in the price of dating long distance. We'd already done that for six months. One day, I looked around and I had everything I wanted. I'd always wanted to work in a top news market and Tampa was a good look. I was also head over heels for this beautiful girl from Houston who got away the first time.

Seven months into my new life, I wanted out. First, the job lost its shine. I was promoted within three months, but management refused to give me a raise saying, "I already hired you for more than I would've paid someone in your position anyway." Once you start playing with my money, things go downhill from there.

Then, my happily-ever-after turned into a nightmare. I decided to leave news, but I really needed to find a job first. I thought, "There must be other women who are feeling this way. What can I do to encourage them?"

I'll write a blog, and so I did, which re-railed the plan I had for my entire professional career.

Purpose Reflections

1. What dues do you have to pay en route to your purpose?

_____

_____

_____

_____

_____

_____

_____

_____

_____

_____

_____

_____

_____

_____

_____

_____

_____

_____

_____

_____

_____

_____

2. What do you feel that you have to prove?

_____

_____

_____

_____

_____

_____

_____

_____

_____

_____

_____

_____

_____

_____

_____

_____

_____

_____

_____

_____

_____

_____

_____

_____

3. Who are you trying to convince that you are successful?

_____
_____
_____
_____
_____
_____
_____
_____
_____
_____
_____
_____
_____
_____
_____
_____
_____
_____
_____
_____
_____
_____
_____
_____

– 9 –
BRAND NEW PATH

Journalism is probably the only profession in the country that employs people who fervently seek to expose lies, injustice, and disparity in other industries but damn near pops a vein in their mostly white, male heads when any of their own improprieties are even discussed.

I learned that the hard way in 2015.

I lived in Tampa and was just over working nine-hours shifts with a 20-minute break. I was done working through lunch, timing my bathroom breaks so I could race to the snack machine and get back to my desk in time to be ignored.

Earlier in my career, I had made two professional decisions. One was not to be an on-air reporter. I chose to be a producer, which meant I not only got to run the show but shape it and had a pretty good run. But there were still challenges. So, when I attended a camp in the mountains of Whitefish, Montana and was asked to reflect on a time I felt "other," I thought, "That's easy." I felt "other" every single day. This is what I wrote:

> *The most exhausting days in the newsroom are the days when I feel no one sees me. The days when I pitch a story and it gets shot down because we just have to do another one-minute 30second story about the gun shop owner selling "Muslimfree" lawn signs. The most disheartening days are the ones when someone enters the newsroom seeking answers from anyone who doesn't look like me.*

Those are the days when I feel invisible; the days when all the bullets on my résumé fade away. They only want to hear from someone white, male, and breathing. My experience no longer matters.

Before I pulled up LinkedIn to skim over jobs outside of journalism, I emailed my mentors. They all answered with the same comforting tone, assuring me that my frustration was normal. It turns out they had all been frustrated with their positions at some point and that's when they knew to move on. I walked away from those conversations with three main points.

Know yourself. The advice you get from other people is just that. People can go on and on all day about how they handled a situation, but you have to make those decisions for yourself.

Know your goals. Remember what you wanted when you first started out in this business. Those goals may have changed along the way, but stay the course. Don't let people deter you from your purpose.

Know that you are needed. In 2012, the National Association of Black Journalists Diversity Census on Media Management found that diversity was on the decline. The same year, the American Society of News Editors found that journalists of color make up about 12 percent of print newsroom staffs. As we know, diversity is about more than having different shades of brown in the editorial meeting. It's about having people on your staff who not only look different, but who challenge thinking by exposing people to different lifestyles and experiences.

In 2007, I decided not to be a television reporter. I chose producing. It's a decision that
puts me on the path to management. I forfeited my dreams of Oprah hair and Diane
Sawyer sit-downs so I could be the person inside the newsroom making those decisions.
Most importantly, I wanted to be a voice for the people. I assured my fellow broadcast
journalism students that I would be a news director one day, and then I would hire them.
I've decided to stick it out because I still want to be that person. As the only black
producer in my station, I see great need for more faces like my own. I also see a need for
you.

After this post, I started hearing from men and women all over the country saying, "Thank you." My editors from the JAWS board loved it, but that was not the case for everyone. A few other sites shared the blog, and my company didn't seem to like it at all. I was called into human resources and asked questions like, "Are you happy here?" and "Is there anything we can do to make the work environment better for you?" Whoa! I didn't think it was that serious. Plus, there's no temporary remedy to an institutional problem.

This was a column about my frustration with the industry, yet my managers were offended.

The work environment changed for me a lot after that post. All of a sudden, I was getting called into the managers' offices every other day. My anxiety was so bad about what they might say about my show that I would wake up with stomach pains. And once I got to work, I'd spend another 20 minutes in a private stall just trying to get my emotions together. The job was eating me alive.

I started going to therapy. It had been far too long since I talked to someone professionally, but between my relationship and my job, I needed an escape.

My personal life was also deteriorating. We'd been having conversations about marriage, but I was starting to think it was all talk. When I came back from a three-day board meeting in Denver, I knew things would be different between us. We barely talked when I was away. When she said she wanted to take a break, I knew that meant forever. Seven days after we broke up, my job decided not to renew my contract.

> **The HR Lady:** "Per section blah blah of your contract, the company is exercising its right not to renew your contract."

> **Me:** OK

> **The HR Lady:** "We're going to need your badge and we need you to leave the building right now."

> **Me:** May I ask why?

> **The White Guy:** We don't have to tell you.

Yes! "The White Guy!" That's all he was to me. He'd proven on more than one occasion that he had no respect for me. I spent way too much time managing up with him and I was tired.

What did I do to him? Why is he so angry? Oh, that's right, I gave voice to the reality of my experience and this was his response.

The HR Lady: Do you have any personal items?

Me: I don't have anything here. Just my purse.

Suddenly, the purse I left downstairs 90 seconds ago appeared at the door.

Who was this mystery delivery person? Did everyone know this was happening?

I had just spent 60 minutes in the morning editorial meeting, which was about 30 minutes too long. Nothing was different for me. In spite of management's attempts to intimidate me, my behavior never changed.

I never stopped pitching stories.

I never stopped checking in with my reporters.

I never stopped coaching my anchors through new choreography for my newscasts.

I never stopped writing my ass off.

I knew they were out to get me, and I never stopped performing.

But now it began to sink in.

Fired? Did I just get fired?

The answer was: yes.

Did I just get fired for posting a blog that encouraged non-whites, non-males to believe in themselves.

Well, yes.

Finding a job after that was hard. Essentially the blog post got me black-balled in broadcasting.

Once again, I had to rebuild myself and my life. I didn't want to face it, but I was on the edge of a depression that I'd yet to experience. In spite of our breakup, Makayla and I were still living together. She only moved across the hall.

I didn't want to leave the house, but I knew I had to bounce back. I did interviews all over, I even flew to New York on my own dime to interview with a top network. I made it beyond the final round. I made it the, "you applied for that job, but we want to give you this job" round, but that didn't last long. The news director came in and shut down the whole process. She said it was too close to my blog for her to hire me.

Don't even get me started.

Then the divine rerouting for my life began. I'd been working with this attorney in Clearwater who fed me exclusive stories. She reached out on my last day at the station and when I told her I no longer worked there, she said she had a job for me.

In 2017, I wrote about the angel who helped me in my "Too Dope Queens" blog series where I featured 31 Black female entrepreneurs who inspired me. This is what I wrote:

> *Long before we bonded over garlic crabs and all things ratchet, we were bonded by love.*

In the most heartbreaking chapter of my life, Michele Rayner Whitfield helped me turn the page. When giving is your ministry, you will always be blessed.

We first met through Facebook. Because we have fifty 'leven mutual friends, "The Book" thought we should be friends, too.

Our relationship quickly escalated past liking posts and random shares. Michele became "the plug." She would feed me exclusive stories to pitch to my news station. We had a great setup and the bosses really love a producer who can produce more than just teases and headlines.

One day Michele reached out about a story involving the death of three teen girls in St. Petersburg. Dominique Battle, age 16, Ashaunti Butler, age 15, and

66

I'M NOT TRYING TO GET YOU TO CHURCH; I'M TRYING TO WAKE UP THE CHURCH INSIDE OF YOU.

– GEORGIA DAWKINS –

EVERYBODY
KNOWS:
THE POWER OF BEING IN POSITION

Laniya Miller, age 15, were found dead inside a car that drove into a pond on March 31, 2016. The sheriff's office said the Honda was reported stolen the night before. To this day, the circumstances surrounding their deaths after a police chase on a dark highway remain a mystery. It was the last story I wrote before being laid off the next day.

When Michele reached out to pitch a different angle, I regretfully confessed that I was no longer with the company. Six days after one of the worst days of my life, she hired me as her media consultant.

Natasha Winkler was the first mother I interviewed. We were preparing her statement for the press conference and I was terrified. My goal was to be delicate with her grief. I didn't push her. I just asked her to introduce me to Laniya, a young woman that I would never have the chance to meet. Natasha's strength inspired me. She was determined to tell the whole truth about her daughter's childhood.

The next day, I beamed with pride as I watched her paint a beautifully tragic picture of her baby girl. I cried in the car.

Because of my experience working on this case, I am not only a better journalist, I am a better person. Michele gave me that opportunity.

In 2016, I fell on hard times more often than I can count, but when I moved away, Michele remained a friend. She's always there to offer a prayer or write a check. She is the friend I never knew I needed.

When I look at Michele, I know that Ashaunti, Dominique, and Laniya are proud. She not only fights for them, she fights for the troubled girl inside of me.

Michele, you are too dope for words.

Just a few days after our first press conference, I got an email about a job in Atlanta. It sounded like a job I would describe as perfect for me. It was. Just not in the ways I imagined.

Purpose Reflections

1. What have you learned from loss?

_____

_____

_____

_____

_____

_____

_____

_____

_____

_____

_____

_____

_____

_____

_____

_____

_____

_____

_____

_____

_____

_____

_____

_____

2. Who does your purpose serve?

_____

_____

_____

_____

_____

_____

_____

_____

_____

_____

_____

_____

_____

_____

_____

_____

_____

_____

_____

_____

_____

_____

_____

_____

_____

_____

– 10 –

A BLOG THAT OPENED DOORS

"That blog got you that job."

My girl Tree had convinced me that the very thing that got me fired had been a set up for my destiny the whole time. Tree was a director when I worked at KSLA. She's not like a best friend at all; she's like a sister. The sister you never asked for, but God assigned you to each other anyway. She was also one of the few people who called daily just to make sure I was alive after I lost my job in Tampa. After allowing me to live in her home for a year, I'd say she knew me better than most people who think they know me but couldn't tell you my middle name. Tree kept me laughing, with comments like, "If I had a house phone, I'd slam it in your face." More importantly, she provided the type of support I needed at a time I felt abandoned.

She once told me, "You're being talked about in rooms you're not even in."

I sure enough didn't talk myself into this.

The job interview in Atlanta meant travel money I didn't have. I did have loyal family. My mama drove me to Atlanta and paid for every drop of gas along the way. She knew I didn't have any money and that taking this job meant taking a step back, financially.

The eight-hour drive seemed even longer with Sway in the car. His real name is Garnett, but I prefer Josue, Sway for short. He's my youngest brother and kinda like my son. He was born when I was 17, which makes me feel more like a teen parent. My point is he's a kid and when you don't have children, they just seem to make everything feel a little longer.

I moved to Atlanta in June, 2016, two months after being escorted out of the newsroom in Tampa, and I've yet to look back.

That night, the three of us slept in my cousin's spare room on her pullout couch. There was nowhere to roll and nowhere to hide. Then reality set in: *This was my bed and I had made it for myself.*

At work I realized the enormity of what had to be done. When I was finally introduced to the show, it was like eating ice chips. It had absolutely no flavor. The executives were referring to it as "Girl Talk" even though it was targeting African-American women. It didn't even have a cultural identity at the time or even any basic cultural knowledge.

First of all, you ain't never 'bout to call a panel of Black women "girls."

I thought I would be joining the production in progress, but I was there from the beginning. The team consisted of creator, the show's two executive producers, and me. I was the only full-time black person on the team. It was my first-time casting talent, but once we narrowed down our favorites, we needed to move to the next step, which was actually developing the show. That was a lot of work.

> *It needed a name.*
> *It needed content.*
> *It needed segments.*
> *It needed colors.*
> *It needed graphics.*
> *It needed hosts.*

The show needed a lot more than what they were paying me to do. I worked for $100 a day, and it took more than 30 days to get my first check. There were no interns and the help we were able to find was borrowed talent from other shows in the building.

For two months, I sat next to "the boss." I watched her every move. I knew when she had to take her medication, I knew when she had a doctor's appointment, and I even knew when her cat was sick. But more than anything, I drew from her years of successful broadcast sales and management experience. I learned how to sell a show.

I hadn't had a white female mentor since Tallahassee. I was intrigued. I think it's important to have mentors who don't use the same brush, comb, or bathroom that you use. I believe these relationships prepare you the most for real world experiences. I welcomed the environment I was in.

During development, I had to come up with dozens of names for the show. It had to be a name that was hip but not too "black." We conducted unofficial focus groups among our friends and women in the building to see which name worked. The one that was my first choice came out on top.

What a relief!

In six weeks, I went from producing auditions to producing rehearsals and from rehearsals to crafting the show pilot. We needed an audience of 30, but since we didn't have the budget for a casting company, we were about twenty short. I came through again and filled the audience with fellow alumni and family members.

Having my older cousins in the room was a huge deal for me. To them, I was always the little cousin who just wanted to hang out with the big girls. I'd never had the big girls come out for me before. In preparation for the pilot, I secured three days of catering, five hours of valet, and a few dozen guests.

Because what's a talk show without guests?

After the pilot was the waiting game. We shot in August. September. October. November. December. January. February. March. The days on the calendar were just peeling away until it finally fell on April. By the time I got the call, I'd just given up. Literally. The night before my phone rang, I called my best friend Camille.

"Is it crazy that I don't even want it anymore?"

"No, it's not crazy," she said.

"I'm just so tired." Waiting was exhausting and I'd lost steam. "Maybe this show was just the opportunity that brought me to Atlanta. I did my job. Maybe God has something else for me to do."

The news came almost one year to the day that I had been laid off in Tampa. That's when I knew the show was getting picked up. I waited two additional months before finally being offered a job. This is what the saints call "trusting the process," but I actually had an advantage. Someone on the inside at another network confirmed the green light.

The day after that call to Camille, the show's creator made an offer.

Here we go again.

I knew the money wasn't enough from the beginning, but I was so desperate for the opportunity that I didn't bother with a counter offer. As far as resources, I was prepared for whatever came my way. I had produced the pilot with impossible staffing, so the next round couldn't phase me.

This time, though, I had help. This time I had a team. Our production team consisted of nine people. If we include the hosts and glam squad, we were an army of 20. We were small but mighty! We started off with three producers. Each of us was responsible for booking, writing, and editing. A few weeks into rehearsals, they added another member to the team. It still wasn't sufficient, but it was more than we had.

"

I WAS SO CONSUMED WITH
EVERYTHING HAPPENING
AROUND ME THAT
I IGNORED WHAT WAS HAPPENING
WITHIN ME.

— GEORGIA DAWKINS —

EVERYBODY
KNOWS:
THE POWER OF BEING IN POSITION

We welcomed phenomenal guests like Avery* Sunshine, Karyn White, Wendy Williams, Marlon Wayans, Vivica A. Fox, Jasmine Guy, Victoria Rowell, and Stephanie Mills, the star of the Wiz' original Broadway production who went viral for her comments about music appropriation on the show. When asked about the state of music, this legend responded, "I think they want R&B but they don't want it from us."

One of our first guests was gospel artist Erica Campbell, who prayed over our show after her interview. I will always treasure the prayer circle she led in the middle of our studio. I remember feeling grateful. I was holding Erica's hand thinking, "This is what I've always wanted."

For the first time in my life, I got a chance to be unapologetically Black, spiritual, and creative. This daily, live black-oriented talk show was freedom to me until it wasn't. Sometimes the miracle you pray for ends up being the thing that pushes you into your destiny.

I reached that point less than a year after starting this new phase in my life, but after the heartaches and trauma of my short time on earth, I had learned one lesson. I knew when it was time to move.

Purpose Reflections

1. What new opportunities can you breathe life into?

_____

_____

_____

_____

_____

_____

_____

_____

_____

_____

_____

_____

_____

_____

_____

_____

_____

_____

_____

_____

_____

_____

2. How much is your purpose worth?

_____
_____
_____
_____
_____
_____
_____
_____
_____
_____
_____
_____
_____
_____
_____
_____
_____
_____
_____
_____
_____
_____
_____
_____

– 11 –
QUITTING MY DREAM JOB

There are times in our lives when we have to get an important message from someone we don't like. Unfortunately, many of us miss vital information because we don't like the source. I keep a mental list of people to tune out as soon as they start talking. My cousin is one of those people.

For the most part, I ignore everything she says. In my mind, she's the selfish cousin. There are other members in my family who would say that's my role. The truth is, we can both be pretty selfish at times, but for the sake of this story, it's her. She's the reason our girl group, Jet Style, broke up back in the '90s. She always wanted to sing lead and stand in the middle while I was the one who wrote all the songs. She got upset because she wholeheartedly believed that she was the one true star. That's girl stuff. What wasn't was the time she called the police on me when I was 11 because I wouldn't be her friend.

Age eleven was hard, mostly because it wasn't the only time I ran from the cops.

That's another story from an earlier part of my life. Right now, it's 2018 and I realize that what I'm hearing is unusual. I want to write it off as her just doing what she does to get attention, right? But I can't do that. Not this time. Her tone was different. Her statement wasn't about judgment or stealing the spotlight. It was about getting my attention. God was using her and that's something I thought that He would never do.

You see, I had given birth and she told me I was supposed to leave my child.

OK, my 'child' was actually a live-broadcast five-day-a-week talk show; but getting it on the air felt like birth to me.

When my cousin told me, I could do better than my dream job, I called her everything but a child of God.

"You think this show is a big deal?" she asked. "You can do so much better than that."

"Are you kidding me right now?!?" I said as I jumped off the couch. "I built this show and you expect me to walk away?"

"Exactly."

I knew she was speaking truth because I also knew my 'baby' was killing me.

People in regular work environments don't know the stress that comes in the broadcast world. Just think of this. You have to hit your deadline *(no one can say wait a minute, we need to start in five minutes)*. Your materials have to be in place *(oh – I'm sorry on-air talent - you can't ask any questions to the city mayor because I forgot to write them)*. And you have to research, book, back-time, write, lead, follow, direct, and literally do hundreds *(I'm not exaggerating)* of tasks every single day – just so you can sit back and watch four people talk on your TV screen for an hour every day. It's great when it's ABC network, or even TMZ. There are hundreds of people assigned to do the various jobs necessary. I worked with nine people on my show in Atlanta and they were beginning to drop like flies. I didn't want to be part of the body count, but it wasn't looking good.

My hands are shaking, but I cannot ask for help. My team is already inundated with tasks and I do not have time to stop and teach someone something that could save me time down the road. I have to keep pushing or I will fall apart.

I came into work early because I knew I had a lot on my plate. It wasn't until 3 hours later that I realized all of the responsibilities before me were just too much. I can handle a lot. I was reared in newsrooms with tight budgets and small staffs, so I know all about making it work – but this? This was too much, and I wasn't built for it.

I'd been filling in for a producer who finally got a few days off. I wanted her to enjoy her time away, so I tried not to call on her. Then, she hit a 102-degree fever, which forced her to stay at home one more day.

I was terrified.

We'd already lost one producer that week and whenever someone was out of the office that always meant more work for me.

Time is racing, but I feel like I'm barely getting anything done. Every time I looked at the clock, another 20 minutes has passed.

I thought I could do it. I thought I could be her, be me, and still be great, but that wasn't in the cards.

Ten minutes before the show, I felt my eyes welling up with tears. I tried finding refuge in one of the private restroom stalls, but they were full. I then ran to my friend's desk in hopes of unloading some of this stress, but she was preoccupied. I could see that she was on a call as I approached her desk, so I kept it moving. At this point, I'm only getting more and more frustrated.

I'm losing time.

With about seven minutes until show time, I head to the booth. I log in, check my graphics, and begin to load my social media elements. I'm just trying to keep busy to avoid erupting and that's when the wardrobe assistant walked in to run prompter.

I told you staffing was tight.

She sat down next to me, looked at my face and asked, "Are you OK?"

Tears came instantly but I didn't want anyone to know that I was losing my grip.

"I can't do this," I whispered.

It took every ounce of energy to force sound past the lump in my throat. "I can't do this. It's too much. It's too much. It's too much."

"Georgia!"

I wiped my face as the clock continued to run. We are now less than two minutes away from the show just in time for my executive producer to walk in with her morning routine.

"Good morning, sports fans!"

I say nothing.

"Georgia, are you OK? Are we good?" she asked.

"No, I'm not OK."

Then, the supervisor in my headset echoes her question.

"Hey Georgia! Are we good to go? Are you OK?"

"No, I'm not OK and I think I need to leave after the show."

I couldn't believe I said those words out loud.

"Are you serious?" the supervisor asked.

"I'm dead serious."

They stood down and for the next 57 minutes and 50 seconds, I was quiet. I was no longer present. My body was there and I could hear myself counting. The show was still on the air, but I don't know how. The only thing on my mind was staying calm long enough to run out the door.

At 9:57:50, my executive producer turned to me with her arms open wide and invitation in her eyes.

In what seemed like a stern whisper, I begged, "Please don't hug me right now."

She backed away.

I placed my headset on the counter and calmly searched for a safe place to cry.

That day was five months after my creation hit the air.

"Good morning. It's Georgia," I said to my therapist in an empty stairwell. "I really need to see you today." I cried. "I need to come right away."

Yes, I'm a strong black woman with a therapist. I know I need help. That's what makes me strong.

My therapist gave me her earliest appointment, which happened to be three hours from that call.

Don't panic.

I looked down. My hands were shaking too badly to walk back into the office, so I sent my boss a text.

"I need a minute."

I knew I needed more than just a minute, but that's all my fingers would let me type.

My plan was to hide out in the locker room, which is the most secluded place in the building, but I didn't make it. I was passing by a friend's office when I stopped at her door. She signaled with her hand to come in, but I could barely take two steps before collapsing in her arms.

The tears wouldn't stop coming. The shaking in my hands sped up and all of a sudden, I was gasping for air. I felt my body shutting down.

"What's wrong? What happened?"

Whimpering I replied, "It's. Just. Too. Much. I. Can't. Do. It. All."

"Wait a minute . . . the show has you like this?"

I nodded.

"Oh, no! You gotta go!" urged my friend.

"I can't leave," I said sobbing. "We have a taping with Kim Fields at noon."

"SO WHAT?!?"

"No one can do it but me," I said.

"They will have to figure it out because you can't stay here."

She calmed me down long enough to email the human resources director and get someone to bring my things.

"Sky, where are you?" She was a young production assistant I'd mentored for nearly two years.

"I'm at my desk," she said.

"I need you to get my things."

"What are you talking about?" she asked.

"Listen, I need you to go into the office, get my coat, my bag and my badge but leave the computer. Then meet me upstairs."

When she found me, there was fear all over her face.

"Georgia, what's going on? What happened? Are you coming back? I can't lose you. You're my big sister."

I hugged her and said, "Everything is going to be OK."

I didn't believe a word that came out of my own mouth.

In between emails and calls about my belongings, I asked my boss to meet me upstairs. I'd hijacked a conference room from the national newspaper chain that also shared the building.

I waited. I watched my bag and I watched the door in anticipation for the moments to come.
I sat, wrapped in my favorite scarf with my jacket already buttoned. I had no idea what I was about to say, but, as it turns out, I didn't have to do much talking.

To my surprise, my boss had also invited my supervisor. She said they both realized some things had gone wrong that day and they wanted a chance to explain how they would fix those problems. I listened without expression. It's as if I was numb. They kept going on and on about putting too much on me, coupled with promises of getting the team more help.

As far as I was concerned, they had already failed. They were still thinking the problem was today. Not. The problem had been all the days leading up to this.

"Georgia, I know I don't tell you this enough, but I really appreciate you," said my supervisor.

This was the same woman who had challenged my judgment and professionalism the entire seven months we had worked together.

"You are the heart and soul of this show and you've been holding us together for a long time. If there is anything you need, personally or professionally, let me know," my supervisor added before leaving the room.

This was not the first panic attack, but my second episode in three weeks. I knew, it was time to go. After all, I had gotten a confirmation through a strange source – my cousin.

"Listen," I interrupted. "I just called you up here to say I am leaving today, and I don't know if I will be back tomorrow, but I'll let you know by three o'clock."

After therapy, I sent an email letting them know I would be out sick the following day.

Later that night, I got a call from human resources asking what it would take to get me to stay. In that moment, I recognized the power that I had all along. They needed me but it was too late. What happened next is still happening. I began to transition into the next phase of my professional life, which has a lot of faith-walking attached to it. It started with a cocoon of emotional support that I had probably taken for granted, but it always seemed to appear in my times of emotional need.

After that call from HR, one of my cousins stayed with me until I fell asleep.

The next day, I got the oil and prayed over my house. Emotions and spirit are tied. I needed healing in both.

Then, my best friend Roxanne and her husband Tony came. They stayed for two nights and Roxanne made sure I left the house. She brought an extra outfit from her trip to Dubai so that I didn't have an excuse to skip a close friend's baby shower. It was good getting out of the house, but I still had anxiety about going back to work. Tony and his friend lit up the fireplace, but it was hard keeping it going. While the guys were out gathering twigs, I took another step toward cleansing my life. Roxanne and I start burning my old documents dating back to 2011.

Why was I holding on to all this stuff?

As I watched the blaze burn up old bills, letters, and board notes I started to cry. Then Roxanne asked, "What's wrong?"

"I'm just so emotional," I said. "I don't know what to do."

But God did. What I didn't need was to be alone.

On Sunday morning, I went to church. Roxanne and Tony got a hotel room. I had every intention on staying home alone, but then another friend called. She invited me over for dinner and suggested I stay with her and her husband for the night. I rested that night like I was on summer vacation. When I woke up, her husband said he'd made me breakfast.

"It's upstairs," he said. "I'll bring it down."

I was staying in their fully furnished downstairs apartment. It was the perfect hideaway.

No one would ever look for me here.

He walked back down with cheese grits, scrambled eggs, grilled chicken breast, toast topped with grape jelly, a glass of ice-cold orange juice, and a bottle of water.

"You didn't have to do this." I said as I admired the incredible spread.

"Of course, we did," he replied. "You're family."

"Thank you," I whispered.

When the door closed behind him, I burst into tears. How could a simple act of love make me so emotional?

I didn't know that it was just the beginning of a day of divine emotional treats for me.

The next came when I returned a phone call.

I'd been meaning to call Sheldon ever since I ignored his call three days prior. But it took me a minute to get my emotions together before I did. Sheldon works for a superstar. You don't know her name, yet, but she's just one of those people. Everything she touches glows. Everyone she touches finds glory in their lives. Officially, Sheldon is her makeup artist, hair stylist, and creative director. He's a master at what he does, but he's so much more than that. He has the gift of discernment and on this day, he came to me as an emissary.

When the phone rang Friday, I watched in fear afraid the call was about the show I was leaving. It took 20 minutes for me to calm down. After leaving my friend and her husband, I tried calling his number, but Sprint swiftly redirected my call to Financial Services.

As soon as I was able to make a payment arrangement, my phone rang, and it was Sheldon.

What are the odds?

"I'm in the neighborhood," said the sultry voice on the other end. "Can I stop by?"

"Sure," I replied knowing he'd never been to my home before.

"Send me the address."

Once he got there, I explained why I ignored his call on Friday. I tried to explain all the drama, but it was making me tired.

"I don't know if I can go back there," I said. "I just don't think I can walk through the door."

"What are you going to do?"

"I guess I'm going to look for something else."

"

PLAY BY THEIR RULES
UNTIL YOU CAN AFFORD
TO MAKE YOUR OWN.

– GEORGIA DAWKINS –

EVERYBODY
KNOWS:
THE POWER OF BEING IN POSITION

Then I thought aloud, "What do you think your boss would say if I told her I'm supposed to work for her?"

He laughed and, "You have no idea how highly she thinks of you."

I studied his face for answers completely unaware of God's next step in His plan for my life.

Purpose Reflections

1. What are you willing to sacrifice in order to passionately pursue your purpose?

_____

_____

_____

_____

_____

_____

_____

_____

_____

_____

_____

_____

_____

_____

_____

_____

_____

_____

_____

_____

_____

2. What does your purpose look like? Where are you?
What is your role? Who are you serving?

_____

_____

_____

_____

_____

_____

_____

_____

_____

_____

_____

_____

_____

_____

_____

_____

_____

_____

_____

_____

_____

_____

_____

– 12 –
FAITH IS

God is time and only He can change things in the blink of an eye. When someone hurts us, it takes us some time to heal, but when something is going right, we start thinking, "It's only a matter of time before this goes south." But God is time. He is then and He is now. Now! And, right now He wants us to focus on what that means.

Snap your fingers.

Do you feel how fast that happened?

Now blink.

Blink again because you missed it the first time.

That's how fast God moves.

How can you not love a God like that? That's the whole reason we pray.

We cry out solemnly asking, "Lord, when is it going to be time? When is it going to be my time?"

Then we beg God saying, "Lord, I just need a little more time."

And sometimes we go to Him with regret. "God, if I could turn back the hands of time . . ."

We also hope.

"God, if I could just see her one more time . . ."

We are the ones who need time, but only He can give it to us. And only He can change it for us.

My time was up at the show I helped create.

I had tried to pretend it wasn't. But it was time to go. It was also time to shed the skin of insincerity that had held me back at previous times in my life. Authenticity has not always been my friend.

For too long, I tried to please the people around me. I did it for the teachers who wanted me to make the grade, the coaches who wanted me to make the play, and the kids at school who just wanted me to give them a show – so I did. I tried to be a good quiet little colored girl for employers, and I played to everyone's desire until my body shut down. But now I'm ready.

And now I'm listening to a messenger tell me about what God has prepared for me. I'm watching his mouth move, but it's taking me a little too long to catch on to what he is actually saying.

"What you don't know is she has her own production company," he said, "and she needs someone to help her build it from the ground up."

Why is he telling me this?

"She just closed on a building a couple days ago," he added.

That's convenient.

"You should call her," he tells me. "You better call her tomorrow because I'm going to call her tonight."

"Do you know what you just said?" I asked him.

He couldn't possibly know that he had just given me the hope I've been looking for in all the wrong things: wrong friendships, wrong apps, wrong job, etc.

"I know who I am," he said in his calm steady voice. "I am a special agent. I know why I'm here. I've been put here to make sure everyone's life is better when I leave it."

He hadn't eaten, so I offered him some of the food I prepared for dinner.

That's when the divine made the entire meeting cross from the probable into the incredible. The friend I'd invited inside my home was sitting at my table in the flesh and all of a sudden, he began speaking to my spirit.

"I'm scared," I said.

"You're not scared," he shook his head. "You've been here before," said the Spirit.

Only God knew that I'd been in this position before in New York City, in Tallahassee, in Fort Myers, in

Shreveport, and in Tampa. Each time, God revealed to me when it was time to go. Some exits came naturally and in others I stayed a little too long.

Do I stay on this job? Or, do I obey the voice of God?

Then, I thought, "This could be the devil. He knows things about us, too."

That's when God started speaking to things in my life that no one knew about. No one knew because I never said them out loud. At this point, I'm convinced that this was the voice of God speaking through the man in front of me, but I also know few people are going to believe me.

"I hope you don't mind if I take a few notes," I told him while shaking my head in amazement.

I opened my notebook and readied my pen because I knew I needed to write these things down. This would be the part of the movie that never happened. When you flash back to this scene, I'll probably be talking to an empty chair, writing quotes no one heard but me.

God told me I had to quit my job. He'd been telling me for months, but I was afraid. I was afraid of failing. I was afraid of being broke. I was afraid of people no longer needing me because I wasn't affiliated with the show.

My whole life I've been told not to question God, but I had a lot of questions and it seemed like a great time to have a conversation.

Me: People aren't going to understand why I'm leaving my dream job. This was highly publicized. Maybe we should reconsider.

God: If you don't move when I tell you to move, you're gonna mess some people up, and if you stay too long, it can be catastrophic.

Me: But God, this was my dream job.

God: This <u>was</u> your dream job, but I've always had bigger and better dreams for you.

I started to think about my career.

I've totally been here before.

Sometimes it's the end of a contract or the end of a season, but I've been here. God has had to move me before.

When I wanted an internship, God gave me a job.

When I wanted local news, God gave me network.

When I wanted to work in a top market, God gave me Top 10.

Then, He gave me a talk show.

He always puts me in the right position. It may not be comfortable, but it's perfect.

I'm sitting at my dining room table staring at this man in disbelief. I keep putting my hand over my mouth because I can't keep it closed. There is no way he could know all of these things.

He looked at me and started to cry.

"Georgia, I don't even see your face anymore. I just see lights. I see lights all over your face."

"Dude, you gotta stop," I said. "This is making me feel crazy."

I got up to put the dishes away and he started praying.

"God, thank you for allowing me to be a vessel for Georgia tonight. Thank you for using me. Thank you for allowing me to be here in her home and break bread with her in her kitchen."

I'm now staring at him like he just took off all of his clothes. I'd never witnessed this kind of humility before. This is normally the prayer and the cry I save for the car.

When I finally regained my composure, I took my seat. "So, how do I do it? How do I quit?"

He said, "If His spirit agrees with the decision, He will direct the course."

Are you kidding me right now? All of that and he answers in riddle!

Then he said, "God did all of this to get your attention. This whole production was just to get your attention. That's how much He loves you."

Production was the perfect word for God to use. Whether it was developing the concept of the show I was about to leave, the divine intervention I'd just witnessed that night, or my entire life, it has all been a production.

"God rerouted my whole day for me to be here with you tonight," he said. "I was supposed to be in Columbus tonight, but God brought me here."

When he walked out of the door, I felt refreshed like when it's 105 degrees at the theme park but then you walked through a cooling mist. That mist was everything! That mist was life abundantly.

He was gone, and I knew what I had to do. Then a text came.

"Girl, please tell me so I know what to expect," wrote a producing friend. She was one of the few people who checked on me while I was out. Her efforts meant the world to me. It's funny how the people who I expected to show up for me never did.

"I'll see you tomorrow," I replied.

The next morning, I went to the doctor. I knew the stress of the job was making me sick. Two panic attacks in three weeks are more than just warning signs. What else was wrong?

"Your blood pressure is a little higher than I like to see," the nurse said as he tried the other arm.

"I've always been big, but I've never had a blood pressure problem."

He said, "Weight ain't got nothing to do with it. You gotta stop stressing."

"Don't worry about that," I said. "I'm about to take care of that right after I leave here."

He took my blood and I prayed, "God, please don't let it be any more than that."

I made my last drive to work to kiss the show I called "my baby" good-bye.

My favorite security guard was at the gate when I pulled up. I normally don't have time to stop but if Felton is there, he's going to want to talk.

"I haven't seen you in a while," he said as he searched my face for answers, but I was all smiles.

"I just needed some time to rest," I explained.

"Ah, I knew you wouldn't quit without telling me first."

I laughed and drove away.

Was it just me or was the sun just a little bit brighter? The sky even seemed bigger.

I looked at the clock.

Oh no! That's the time my emissary told me to call.

I panicked and prayed one more time.

"God, I think I hear you but I'm not sure you really want me to do what you're asking me to do."

I waited.

"Is the act of faith putting in my notice because you said "quit" or is it calling this lady? Which do I do first?"

Then God said to me, "I told you to do both."

I took the phone off Bluetooth and called her up. I needed something to hold onto during this call because God was blowing my mind.

"Good morning, Georgia!" said the cheery voice on the other end.

What? She never answers when I call. I always get her voicemail.

"Good morning." My nerves were trying to take over, but then I remembered what God promised me.

"This is going to sound a little weird, but just go with it," I swallowed. "I'm sitting outside the studio headed in to give my two weeks' notice because God said you had a job for me."

We both stopped breathing. The silence wasn't long, but it was loud enough to get my attention.

"Oh my gosh, Georgia. I do have a job for you. I've had a job for you. I've just been waiting for you."

She explained that she had a production company and she'd started developing a new show.

Ah! I remember. She said something about a show six months ago at lunch.

We often met up for lunch, but I had no idea that she had been preparing me all along.

"What do you think they're going to say when you walk in there?" she asked.

"They're probably going to try to keep me," I told her.

"Well, just be open. Don't be surprised if they ask you for more time."

Was she serious? She held a job for me and she was willing to wait a little longer? Where did she come from?

"How do you feel?" she asked.

"I feel a lot better now." Then she started to pray.

She prays? Duh, of course she prays. That's how we got here in the first place.

She asked God to give me courage, and she asked Him to cover me.

I walked through the door like Lazarus when he popped up out the grave. Everyone counted me out. No one expected me to come back or at least that's what they told me. I could tell how they really felt by looking at who was calling when I was away. The majority welcomed me back with hugs and kisses and told me how much they missed me.

Little did they know . . .

I put my stuff down and called out to the producer who sent the text the night before. "Can I see you for a minute?"

I pulled her into the same conference room where I'd met the bosses one week prior.

"I'm leaving," I confessed. "I'm putting in my two weeks' notice today."

"Oh no, Georgia! What are they going to do? I'm leaving, too. I just put in my notice right before you walked in."

"I don't know what they're going to do," I replied. "That's no longer our problem."

Wow! Three producers in one week. I guess the stress wasn't all in my head. Other people were taking heed.

It took more than an hour for me to track down the managers. While I waited for them, I pulled one member of the on-air team aside to give her a heads up. She was the true on-air anchor of the show. She couldn't help it. She came from radio. Her voice brings joy to anyone's face and having her on camera is just a bonus. No matter what the climate, she remained consistent. What we did and how we did it was never about her. Everything we did was for the people. I connected with her before we ever met in person. You see, she was also a graduate of FAMU, and my professors had been bragging about her for years. She was someone we all aspired to be. She looked out for me and I looked out for her. Hers was one of the first reels I watched when scouting talent. She was already on the short list. I just had to cosign.

In the hours leading up to taping the pilot, she could sense something wasn't right.

"Are you OK?" she asked.

"I'm fine," I replied, hoping she would go away.

Instead, she pulled me into an empty edit bay, grabbed my hands, and prayed for me. I felt I owed her at least a heads up before I walked out the door.

She was sad at first and then she was happy. She knew I hadn't been happy in a long time and was just glad to see me at peace.

My bosses on the other hand, played it cool. They gave me the typical "We understand," spiel. Then, I was offered more money.

I knew before I walked in the door that it wouldn't be enough.

"It's not about the money, and it's not about my title," I explained.

"It's not even about the people. There will be difficult people everywhere I go," I said as I looked into her eyes across the tiny conference table. "God says I have to go, so I have to go."

She replied, "Well, I understand that." We'd talked about God before, but not like this. We'd only spoken about God in the superhero sense.

I wouldn't be here today if it wasn't for God.

I didn't really expect her to understand what was happening in my life, and she didn't have to.

"Listen Georgia, I am forever indebted to you for helping me create this show, and if there's any way I can help you let me know."

It's amazing how people see your value once they can no longer milk it for all it's worth. I spent the rest of my day letting everyone on my team know that my time with the show was up.

Everyone had the same questions, "Why, Georgia?" and "How could you leave?"

And everyone got the same answer, "Because God said it's time for me to leave."

Only certain people understood right away. Those were the people who God had repositioned a time or two in their own lives. For those who didn't understand right away, God dealt with them.

A friend who worked on the show came to me the next day.

"Georgia, I was selfish yesterday when you were leaving because I don't want you to leave, but then I went home, and I asked God to talk to me like He talks to you."

Two days later, 30 minutes before I was to meet this angel who held a job for me, my dad called. He was mumbling something about me not reading a scripture he gave me.

"It's on my to-do list," I assured him. "I'm going to get to it."

"You were supposed to read it!"

Geesh!

"OK! OK! I'll read it and call you back."

After reading the full chapter, my dad said to me, "Georgia, you have to pray before everything you do . . ."

Noted.

"You have to pray before you step out of bed in the morning. You have to pray before you brush your teeth. Pray before you open a door. You have to pray about everything."

I'm listening, but I'm also checking the clock because I know this is a very important meeting.

"Thanks, Dad! I have to run and meet the lady and I'm still at work. I'll call you back."

We were meeting at Lenox Mall in Atlanta, which made me hasty. I hate going to Lenox Mall as much as I hate driving in Atlanta. I always feel like I'm going to have to fight at any moment. The traffic in that area is New Yorkish. Whenever I am forced to go there, I always park in the same place. It helps me control the situation, but this time, I followed my Dad's advice and prayed.

"Ok, God!" I said unsure if He was actually listening. "Where should I park?"

He then told me to park in the opposite lot of my usual spot. When I pulled in, there were about 50 parking spaces and each one was full.

See! I knew I was crazy. God ain't talking to me.

A car started to back out and I got excited. Then another car pulled in from the opposite entrance to get the spot.

Seriously?

When the second car backed out, I got really happy.

It's a miracle! Two parking spaces at Lenox at the same time.

I backed in and as soon as I shifted the car into park, someone leaned on their horn.

Oh, hell nah!

Now I'm looking around for the person who's about to catch these hands. Just like that, the Georgia from my troubled past reared her head. I'd been looking for a fight for 15 years, and I thought I'd finally found it when I turned to my left.

It was her! The lady who held the job for me. God brought me right to her car door. We were face to face.

She rolled down the window to acknowledge the coincidence.

"We're in sync!" she said smiling. "Give me five minutes."

Oh, now I know God is a comedian. Is He playing games with me? Am I dreaming? This ain't real.

The restaurant where we'd planned our meeting was too loud, so we walked inside the mall. We sat down at a table for two in the middle of a place that felt like sitting in stalled interstate traffic. I had to fill her in. I told her all about the stress, my panic attacks, and the people God used to get me ready for this conversation.

On the day of my most recent breakdown, my dad was speaking into my life. I knew he had a prophetic gift and that was 65 percent of the reason I avoided talking to him. There are some things I just don't want to know.

"Georgia, you're about to take off, and for where you are going, everybody can't go. There are some people who are going to fly off during takeoff. They're not going to be able to hang onto you anymore."

You see why I don't talk to him?

"Be mindful of the people who are standing in your light because that's the only way they can be seen."

Normally, I would have been a little freaked out, but God was telling me the same thing.

Then she started speaking.

Finally! The answers I've been waiting for.

We sat there for four hours. She not only explained how I was going to assist her, but she made a commitment to help me build my brand.

WHAT?!? GEORGIA DAWKINS???

It's funny how purpose works. I showed up eager to help her, and she turned around with the plot twist. God had been positioning me for my destiny since before I was born.

Guess what? I'm ready.

Is this what all the drama of my life was about? Touché, God! Touché!

Purpose Reflections

1. What does faith look like to you?

_____

_____

_____

_____

_____

_____

_____

_____

_____

_____

_____

_____

_____

_____

_____

_____

_____

_____

_____

_____

_____

_____

_____

_____

_____

_____

2. Write out your commitment. What are you going to do to get into position? (It can be a prayer or a letter to yourself).

_____

_____

_____

_____

_____

_____

_____

_____

_____

_____

_____

_____

_____

_____

_____

_____

_____

_____

_____

_____

_____

_____

_____

_____

Final Prayer

"Now faith is the substance of things hoped for, the evidence of things not seen."

— Hebrews 11:1 KJV

Dear *God, please forgive me for not honoring the God in me. You made me in your image and I took it for granted, but I'm ready now. I see the light and I am not afraid. I'll be who you called me to be, and I'll go where you want me to go. Just give me the words that you want me to say.*

You name the time and the place, and I'll be there with my light.

Amen.

Purpose Reflections

Purpose Reflections

Purpose Reflections

Purpose Reflections

Purpose Reflections

Acknowledgements

To my mom, thank you for showing me how to laugh through the pain. To my dad, thank you for showing me how to keep coming back to God. To my brothers, thank you for protecting me. To my sisters, thank you for correcting me. To my community, thank you for investing in me. To my church, thank you for being my very first audience. To my Lord and Savior, thank you for showing me unconditional love. To my readers, let purpose be your guide.

About the Author

Georgia Dawkins is an award-winning author, producer, and journalist. As the Chief Executive Officer of Georgia Dawkins Media, Georgia develops original programming while coaching others on how to break into production. Affectionately known as the "purpose producer," this rising star is committed to empowering communities through media.

From Los Angeles to Atlanta, Georgia has worked on national productions with BET and Entertainment One, and now she is expanding her reach across the country. In 2019, she added the Black News Channel (BNC) to her list of accomplishments when she joined the team as the Director of HBCU Services. In that role, the Florida A&M alumni creates training opportunities and programming for black colleges.

As an aspiring journalist, Georgia got her start with Good Morning America in 2008. Since then, she has gone on to produce television content for millions of viewers around the country. She has served as a television news producer in cities including Tallahassee, Fla., Fort Myers, Fla., Shreveport, La., and Tampa, Fla., all before reaching the age of 28.

In 2012, she was tapped for Gulf Shore Business magazine's 40 Under 40 regional leadership award. She has served on the boards of the National Association of Black Journalists (NABJ) and the Journalism and Women Symposium. In 2018, NABJ honored Dawkins with the

Outstanding Literary Work award for her debut book, *Everybody Knows: The Power of Being in Position.*

Dawkins has a Bachelor of Arts degree in broadcast journalism from Florida A&M University. She also serves on the board of directors of the School of Journalism and Graphic Communications' Board of Visitors, where she helps guide the curriculum for future journalists. Georgia is currently working on her second book set to be released in 2020.

www.ingramcontent.com/pod-product-compliance
Lightning Source LLC
Chambersburg PA
CBHW072152090426
42740CB00012B/2240